In the Beginning, God...

A Study of the Book of Genesis

BY BOB AND SANDRA WALDRON

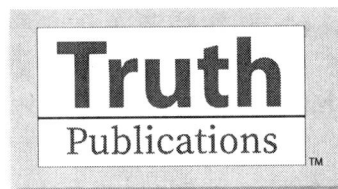

Truth
Publications™

ISBN 10: 1-58427-107-8

ISBN 13: 978-1-58427-107-9

First Printing: 2006

Truth Publications, Inc.
CEI Bookstore
220 S. Marion St., Athens, AL 35611
855-492-6657
sales@truthpublications.com
www.truthbooks.com

Table of Contents

Detailed Outline of Genesis

I. **The Creation Stories (Gen. 1:1-5:32)**
   A. Creation of the Heavens and the Earth (1:1-2:25)
      1. Day one (1:1-5)
      2. Day two (1:6-8)
      3. Day three (1:9-13)
      4. Day four (1:14-19)
      5. Day five (1:20-23)
      6. Day six (1:24-31)
      7. Day seven (2:1-3)
      8. The Garden of Eden (2:4-17)
      9. God makes Eve (2:18-25)
   B. The first sin (3:1-24)
   C. Cain and Abel (4:1-24)
   D. Generations of Adam (4:25-5:32)

II. **The Flood (Gen. 6:1-9:29)**
   A. Mankind becomes wicked (6:1-4)
   B. God warns Noah to prepare for the flood (6:5-22)
   C. The flood begins (7:1-24)
   D. The flood waters recede (8:1-22)
   E. God's covenant with Noah (9:1-17)
   F. A curse is placed upon Canaan (9:18-29)

III. **The Scattering of the People (Gen. 10:1¬11:32)**
   A. The generations of the sons of Noah (10:1-32)
      1. The descendants of Japheth (10:1-5)
      2. The descendants of Ham (10:6-20)
      3. The descendants of Shem (10:21-32)
   B. The Tower of Babel (11:1-9)
   C. The generations of Shem—Narrowed to one line (11:10-26)

> **First Section—1-11**
> Creation Stories: 1-5
> The Flood: 6-9
> Scattering of People: 10-11
>
> **Second Section—12-50**
> Abraham: 12:1-25:18
> Isaac: 25:19-28:9; 35:28-29
> Jacob: 28:10-36:43; 38:1-30
> Joseph: 37:1-36; 39:1-50:26

IV. The Patriarchs (Gen. 11:27-50:26)
  A. Abraham (11:27-25:18)
    1. Generations of Terah (11:27-32)
    2. Abram moves to Canaan (12:1-9)
    3. Abram lies to Pharaoh (12:10-20)
    4. Abram and Lot separate (13:1-18)
    5. Abram rescues Lot (14:1-24)
    6. God's covenant with Abram (15:1-21)
    7. Birth of Ishmael (16:1-16)
    8. Covenant of Circumcision (17:1-27)
    9. The Lord visits Abraham (18:1-15)
    10. Abraham pleads for Sodom (18:16-33)
    11. Destruction of Sodom and Gomorrah (19:1-29)
    12. Lot and his daughters (19:30-38)
    13. Abraham lies to Abimelech (20:1-18)
    14. Birth of Isaac (21:1-7)
    15. Ishmael is sent away (21:8-21)
    16. Abimelech makes a covenant with Abraham (21:22-34)
    17. Abraham offers Isaac (22:1-19)
    18. News from Nahor's family (22:20-24)
    19. Death of Sarah (23:1-20)
    20. Abraham gets a wife for Isaac (24:1-67)
    21. Abraham and Keturah (25:1-6)
    22. Abraham's death (25:7-11)
    23. Generations of Ishmael (25:12-18)
  B. Isaac (25:19-28:9; 35:28-29)
    1. Birth of Jacob and Esau (25:19-26)
    2. Jacob buys Esau's birthright (25:27-34)
    3. Isaac's conflict with the Philistines (26:1-33)
    4. Esau marries Hittite women (26:34-35)
    5. Jacob deceives Isaac (27:1-28:5)
    6. Esau marries a daughter of Ishmael (28:6-9)
  C. Jacob (28:10-36:43; 38:1-30; 48:1-49:33)
    1. Jacob sees God at Bethel and makes a vow to Him (28:10-22)
    2. Jacob meets Rachel (29:1-12)
    3. Jacob serves Laban for Rachel (29:13-20)
    4. Jacob is deceived (29:21-30)
    5. Leah bears children (29:31-35)
    6. Conflicts between Leah and Rachel (30:1-24)

7. Laban pays Jacob wages (30:25-43)
8. Jacob flees from Laban (31:1-55)
9. Esau is coming! (32:1-21)
10. Jacob wrestles with an angel (32:22-32)
11. Jacob and Esau are reconciled (Gen. 33:1-17)
12. Jacob comes to Shechem and buys land (33:18-20)
13. Simeon and Levi smite the men of Shechem (34:1-31)
14. Jacob goes to Bethel (35:1-15)
15. Death of Rachel (35:16-20)
16. Reuben's sin and Isaac's death (35:21-29)
17. The generations of Edom (36:1-43)
18. Judah and Tamar (38:1-30)

D. Joseph (Gen. 37:1-36; 39:1-50:26)
1. Joseph's brothers grow jealous (37:1-11)
2. Joseph is sold into slavery (37:12-36)
3. Joseph is betrayed by Potiphar's wife (39:1-23)
4. Joseph interprets the dreams of the butler and the baker (40:1-23)
5. Pharaoh dreams (41:1-45)
6. Joseph is ruler in Egypt (41:46-57)
7. Joseph's brothers come to buy grain (42:1-38)
8. The brothers return to Egypt (43:1-15)
9. The brothers dine with Joseph (43:16-34)
10. Joseph tests his brothers (44:1-34)
11. Joseph reveals himself to his brothers (45:1-15)
12. Preparations for Israel to move to Egypt (45:16-28)
13. Israel moves to Egypt (46:1-27)
14. Jacob and Joseph are re-united (46:28-34)
15. Joseph introduces his family to Pharaoh (47:1-12)
16. Joseph purchases the land of Egypt for Pharaoh (47:13-26)
17. The time of Jacob's death draws near (47:27-31)
18. Jacob blesses Ephraim and Manasseh (48:1-22)
19. Jacob blesses his sons (49:1-27)
20. The death of Jacob (49:28-33)
21. The embalming and burial of Jacob (50:1-14)
22. Joseph assures his brothers (50:15-21)
23. Joseph's death (50:22-26)

The Bible Story

Only one book in the Bible is made up of short, one line or one paragraph wise sayings, and that is the book of Proverbs. There are many laws and rules in the Bible, but it is not one long checklist of rules to be marked off each day. The Bible is not even a series of unconnected, "once-upon-a-time" stories. It is the unfolding of a beautiful, eternal plan God made for the redemption of mankind. All the little stories fit together to form one beautiful whole.

What would you think of your child's American history teacher if he described the modern space program the first day class met, then he told a story about a man named Columbus the next day, followed by a story about George Washington, and then a description of the development of computers? Suppose he never tied the stories together to make one coherent account of the history of our nation. Even if your child liked his stories, would that erase the fact that the teacher left his class with a very poor grasp of how this country came to be?

In the same way, what if a Bible teacher tells fascinating stories about David today, then Samson next Sunday, followed by Jonah and the whale, and then the baby Jesus? What if he never shows the pupils how the stories fit together? The Bible is the history of God's dealings with mankind. It is the story of the preparation for and the coming of the Christ. Is one a "good" teacher if his pupils sit at his feet week after week—and fail to learn the scheme of redemption?

Have you ever read your Bible in its entirety? What would you think of your school system if you learned it was using teachers who had never had a course in the subject they were due to be teaching? What if the teacher had never read the textbook? The Bible is supposed to be the textbook in any Bible class we teach. Is it important to read a biology textbook before trying to teach it—but unimportant to read the Bible before trying to teach it? Too many people in our world presume to be instant experts on the Bible even though they would not treat any other subject in the world that way.

What should we teach?

The Story of Redemption

"In the beginning..." Come with me back to that point. There is no world, no universe, no physical life, no physical substance, no time. Eternity has no beginning, no end. What did exist? How did all we know come into being? What does it all mean?

There were three Beings in existence who are as everlasting as eternity itself: Jehovah, the Word, and the Holy Spirit. These separate Beings are yet one in purpose, in righteousness, and in deity. They comprise all that is Godhood.

At some point—we have no idea when—lesser heavenly beings were created. We read of innumerable hosts of angels (Rev. 5:11), of seraphim (Isa. 6:2), of cherubim (Gen. 3:24), and of other heavenly creatures around the throne of God (Rev. 4). At some point some of these heavenly beings sinned (2 Pet. 2:4). Again, we do not know the reason. Such matters are the secret things that belong to God (Deut. 29:29). A place of punishment, terrible beyond our comprehension, was prepared for these wicked beings (Matt. 25:41). They were "delivered into chains of darkness, to be reserved unto judgment" (2 Pet. 2:4). These heavenly beings are more powerful than man, but they, as the created, are far less than God the Creator.

"In the beginning" God spoke the physical universe into existence. Then He began placing life on the earth. First

CREATION

came plant life; then fish, fowls, and land animals. The creation process was not yet complete, because there was not yet life that could understand or share a companionship with God. Thus man was created.

"Let us make man in our image" (Gen. 1:26). Man is like God because man can reason, and he has a soul within that will never cease to exist, an essence that is spiritual.

God placed Adam and Eve in a garden of beauty far greater than we can find today. The earth was new and unpolluted. Every desirable plant was there. There were no thorns or thistles; there was no pain or sorrow; there was no anxiety or fear. Adam and Eve had access to the Tree of Life so they need never die. Best of all, they had companionship with God Himself (Gen. 3:8).

But God did not want a creature who was His companion simply because there was nothing else he could do. Then man would have been no more than a robot programmed to worship God, and incapable of anything else. So God gave man a commandment. Adam and Eve were forbidden to eat of the fruit of the Tree of Knowledge of Good and Evil.

There was food in abundance, so hunger did not encourage the eating of the forbidden fruit. The Garden of Eden was so big that a river ran through it and then parted into four heads, so there was no reason for the temptation to be constantly before their eyes. But mankind is easily tempted. When the serpent tempted Eve, she was beguiled and ate of the forbidden fruit. She gave it to Adam and he ate also.

Now they knew shame, guilt, and fear. God gave each guilty party a curse. Pain, sorrow, problems, thorns, death, separation from the Tree of Life—and, worst of all, separation from the companionship of God.

Their sin was no surprise to God. He knew before creation that man could be tempted and He had prepared for man's fall. God had already

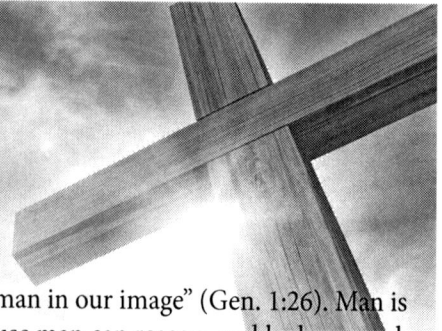

planned how man might be saved (Eph. 3:10-11). By their sin, Adam and Eve gave up the opportunity for complete happiness on this earth. God began the long process of unfolding His plan of how man could live forever with Him, provided man accepted His terms.

Even with this curse, God gave the first glimmer of hope of a day when one of the seed of woman would bruise the head of the serpent (Gen. 3:15). Evil had triumphed on this day with Adam and Eve, but someday man would triumph through the One God would send to complete His plan.

THE FIRST PROMISE OF A SAVIOR

God never for one moment forgot His purpose. Many, many years have passed since that day Adam sinned. The people who have lived cannot be counted. The Bible tells us about only a few of the vast multitude who have lived because they are the ones through whom He unfolded His plan.

Adam lived 930 years and had sons and daughters. The Bible tells a story about Cain and Abel, two of these sons. You remember how Cain became angry and killed his brother because Abel's sacrifice was acceptable to God, and Cain's was not. Abel's death erased his name from further part in the unfolding of God's plan. God takes time in the last of Genesis 4 to tell briefly what happened to Cain and his descendants—then his family is left.

Adam had another son, Seth. We are told nothing about him except that it is through his family that the story develops. About as many years pass during the first five chapters of Genesis as in all the rest of the Bible. God tells us practically nothing about this period because it is unimportant for His purpose to do so. The people typically lived 900 or more years. Among the ten generations named is a man named Enoch. He was righteous, and God highly blessed him by taking him to heaven without dying.

As men spread over the earth, they followed after wickedness on every hand. Their thoughts were only evil continually.

THE FLOOD

God decided to destroy man—except for faithful Noah and his family. Noah accepted God's grace and took the escape offered. He, his three sons, their wives, and two of each form of animal life survived in the ark.

Now we are back to one family, that of Noah's. There are three sons, so no human historian could have known at this point which son to follow, but God guided the writer to follow the line through Shem, touching only briefly the descendants of Ham and Japheth. The writer deals with the nations which came through Ham and Japheth only as they touch Shem's descendants.

Many, many peoples came through Shem, but the divine record narrows the story still more. Years passed, and men no longer lived as long. Soon 200 or fewer years was a long life.

PROMISES TO ABRAHAM:

LAND NATION SPIRITUAL

Some nine generations pass from Noah, and we come to a man named Terah living in Ur of the Chaldees. There were three sons in this family also: Nahor, Abram, and Haran. Haran died while they were still in Ur, and the story follows his son Lot for a while because he traveled with Abram, the more important character.

God called Abram (or Abraham as his name became) and told him to leave his family and to go to a land he would be shown. Abraham obeyed and was led to the little land of Canaan. A three-fold promise was made to him: he was told his descendants would be made a great nation, that nation would inherit the land of Canaan, and, through his seed, all families of the earth would be blessed (Gen.12:1-7). The rest of the Bible is the story of the fulfilling of these three promises.

Notice that God had unfolded only a small part of His plan for man's redemption by this point in history. We know that One will come who will triumph over Satan (Gen. 3:15). We now know further that this One will come from the nation composed of the descendants of Abraham, and that all nations will be blessed by His coming (Gen. 12:2-3).

Abraham's wife was barren so she and Abraham tried to help God fulfill His promise by having a son through Hagar, the handmaiden. Ishmael was born. Abraham later had six other sons by Keturah, another handmaiden. They were blessed because they were sons of Abraham, but these were not the promised seed. Finally, through a miracle, Isaac was born when his father was 100 years old.

When Isaac became head of the family, God repeated the three-fold promise to Isaac: Land, Nation, and Spiritual. Through his seed all nations would be blessed (Gen. 26:2-4).

Isaac had two sons, Esau and Jacob. Even before their birth, God said that Jacob would be the greater. Esau's descendants became the nation of the Edomites. But it was to Jacob that the three-fold promise was repeated. He would receive the land; his descendants would form a great nation; and through his seed all families of the earth would be blessed (Gen. 28:13-14).

JACOB'S TWELVE SONS

Space does not allow us to tell the details of Jacob's life. Suffice it to say that Jacob had twelve sons. He loved Joseph, next to the youngest, best, and showed his partiality. The other brothers were jealous and sold Joseph as a slave into Egypt. There he served as slave to Potiphar; he was lied about and was cast into prison; time passed, and he interpreted Pharaoh's dreams and became ruler of all Egypt, second only to Pharaoh. As he himself said, he was in Egypt to help save life during a severe, seven-year famine (Gen. 45:4-8). You remember how the brothers came, were tested, and finally learned Joseph's identity. Joseph brought all his family to Egypt. There were 75 people in the family at this point—still far short of a nation.

As Jacob lay on his deathbed, he called his sons and gave each a blessing. These sons would form the tribes which would make up the nation of Israel (Jacob was given the name Israel the night he wrestled with an angel). It was to Judah, his fourth son, that he gave a special prophecy. The scepter (the sign of rulership) would not depart from Judah's family until Shiloh—this special One—should come (Gen. 49:10).

Now God has unfolded this much of His plan: One will come to triumph over Satan. He will bless all families of the earth. He will come through the seed of Abraham, through Isaac, through Jacob, and through Judah. He will reign. We know more than we did when Adam sinned, but we still understand very little about God's full purpose (see Gen. 3:15; 12:1-3; 26:2-4; 28:13-14; 49:10).

THE FAMILY IN EGYPT

The book of Genesis closes with Joseph's confident assurance to his brethren that the day would come when God would lead the people back to Canaan. Many years pass before the curtain rises again. Has God forgotten?

The scene looks dark as the book of Exodus begins. By now there are perhaps three million people called Israelites, or Hebrews (later called Jews). A Pharaoh has arisen who does not know Joseph. He feared this vast group of people in his land, so he afflicted them by making them his slaves, but they only multiplied faster. He tried to destroy potential soldiers by ordering the death of all baby boys.

At this very time a baby boy was born. His mother hid him three months and then placed him in the bulrushes at the edge of the Nile. He was found by Pharaoh's daughter, who named him Moses. For forty years he was trained as the son of Pharaoh's daughter. His own mother was hired to care for him, so he grew from babyhood knowing the plight of his people.

At age forty, Moses decided to rescue his people, but God was not ready. Moses killed an Egyptian and had to flee for his life. The next forty years he worked as a shepherd in Midian. Then one day God appeared to Moses in a burning bush and gave him his commission to go back to Egypt to rescue the Israelites.

THE EXODUS FROM EGYPT

Again, space forbids any details. As you remember, Pharaoh refused to let the people go. God showed His might over the most powerful nation of the day by sending ten terrible plagues until the Egyptians were begging the Israelites to leave.

Instead of leading the people directly to the land of Canaan, God directed them southeastward to Mount Sinai. There He made a covenant with them. He promised to be their God and to allow them to be His people if they would obey Him and keep His commandments (Exod. 19:3-9). The people wanted God's blessings and were quick to agree to the covenant. God gave them a law that specified exactly how they were to live as His chosen people.

Until this time, God had spoken directly to the fathers of faithful families. That system (called the Patriarchal system) continued with all people except this special group assembled at Mount Sinai. God was preparing a special people to be ready for the completion of His plan.

God showed His power and protection to His nation in every conceivable way. He fed them when they were hungry; He gave them water from stones; He fought their enemies and shielded them as a father shields his son (Hos. 11:1). But the people did not keep their side of the covenant. Within six weeks of agreeing to obey God and to keep His commandments, they made a golden calf to worship. They murmured when they were thirsty and complained over the manna God had given them for food. Even when they reached Canaan's border, they were too cowardly to go forward as God commanded. They sent twelve spies through the land. Ten brought back word that the task would be too difficult. Only Joshua and Caleb trusted the power of God. The people were forced to turn back to wander forty years in the wilderness, until every soldier above twenty years of age was dead except Joshua and Caleb.

PEOPLE FORCED TO WANDER IN THE WILDERNESS

Exodus, Leviticus, and Numbers give the law of Moses in detail and tell the important events during these forty years. Even Moses disobeyed God on one occasion, and he was not allowed to enter the promised land. God allowed him to view the land from the top of Mount Nebo; then he died and was buried by the hand of God.

The book of Deuteronomy is a series of speeches that Moses made on the plains of Moab just before his death. He was pleading with the people to be faithful when they entered the land, so that they might prosper and might remain in the land through all the generation to follow. God, through Moses, promised great blessings to the people if they would be faithful to Him. On the other hand, He warned of punishments if they turned from Him.

Both sides of the picture—blessings and cursings—are absolutely necessary in God's plan. God has always offered man great blessings for keeping His law and has set stated penalties for disobedience. Then He has left it to man to choose which he wants. Joshua became the leader in Moses' stead and led the people across the Jordan River to conquer the land. They marched around Jericho by faith, and God caused those mighty walls to fall. Joshua and his army found victory on every hand, and, within a very few years, the whole land was conquered and divided among the tribes.

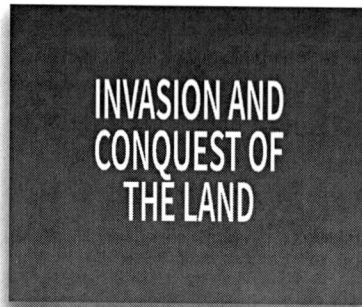

INVASION AND CONQUEST OF THE LAND

Joshua became the leader in Moses' stead and led the people across the Jordan River to conquer the land. They marched around Jericho by faith, and God caused those mighty walls to fall. Joshua and his army found victory on every hand, and, within a very few years, the whole land was conquered and divided among the tribes.

Two of the promises made to Abraham have been fulfilled by this time. Abraham's descendants have indeed become a nation, and God has led them to victory in gaining the land (Josh. 21:43-45). Only the spiritual promise was still lacking. God was still gradually unfolding His plan for mankind to learn, but the "fullness of the times" had not yet come.

The Israelites were faithful to God under the leadership of Joshua and remained so as long as the elders who had served with him lived. But man is weak. As soon as the first victories were over, and each tribe received its portion of land, the soldiers grew lax. They did not drive out the remaining pockets of Canaanites, as God had commanded them. When they failed, God left the Canaanites to prove Israel to see if the nation would be faithful (Judg. 2:3). Israel failed the test. Very little time passed before they turned from God to the idols of their neighbors.

The next period of Israelite history is one of cycles. There was no one single leader during

THE JUDGES

these 400 or so years as there had been under Moses and Joshua. The people would turn to idols; God would allow an enemy to oppress them; they would repent and cry to God for help; then God would raise a judge or deliverer.

There were fifteen such judges. There was Ehud, who killed Eglon king of Moab and led the people to throw off Moabite oppression. There was Deborah, who went with Barak the general to fight against Sisera and the Canaanites. There was Gideon, who defeated the numberless host of Midianites with his tiny army of 300. There was Jephthah, who vowed to sacrifice the first thing which came from his house if he were successful in battle. There was Samson to whom God gave superhuman strength as he served as a one man army against the Philistines.

Our first glance at the period would indicate it was a time of constant warfare. This is disproved, however, by such verses as Judges 3:11, 30, which say the land had "rest forty years" or the land had "rest eighty years."

The little story of Ruth occurs during the period of the Judges. It is a delightful story of a Moabite girl who left her home to follow her mother-in-law to the land of Israel. There she married Boaz, a near kinsman of her dead husband. Is it merely a human-interest story, however? There were other virtuous young ladies in Israel. There were other happy homes. Ruth and Boaz had a son named Obed. He had a son named Jesse, who had a son named David, who had a descendant named Jesus. Ruth was a link in the eternal plan of God!

Eli was priest and judge the day a woman named Hannah prayed earnestly for a son. God granted her wish, and Samuel was born. Hannah dedicated him to God as soon as he was old enough to help Eli around the tabernacle. Samuel is truly one of the names to be added to the list of great characters in the Bible. He judged Israel during a long life span.

When Samuel was old, the people begged for a king. Samuel was distressed, but God told him to give them their king. They had rejected God as their king rather than rejecting Samuel as their judge. Under

God's direction, the young man Saul of the tribe of Benjamin was anointed. Saul was very humble at first, but pride became the ruling attitude of his life. He failed to obey God until finally God rejected his family as the ruling family.

THE UNITED KINGDOM

God sent Samuel to Bethlehem to anoint a son of Jesse as king. Seven of Jesse's sons passed before Samuel, and God turned each one down. Finally the youth David was called from the field and anointed. David was a man after God's own heart (Acts 13:22). There are about 130 chapters in the Bible either relating the history of David or recording the Psalms he wrote. He was human and made mistakes just as other great men have done. Perhaps we are most impressed with his righteousness as we read the psalm of penitence he wrote after his sin with Bathsheba (see Psalm 51).

David wanted to build a temple for God, but God sent Nathan the prophet to tell him that he could not do so because he was a man of war. Instead God promised to let his son build the house. God then promised to establish David's throne forever. If his descendants sinned, God would chasten them with "the rod of men," but He would never remove His mercy from the line of David as He had from Saul (2 Sam. 7:11-16;1 Chron. 17:11-14).

By this point, God has unfolded this much of His plan: One will triumph over Satan; He will bless all families of the earth; this One will come through Abraham, through Isaac, through Jacob, through Judah, and through David. He will reign on the throne of David forever (Gen. 3:15; 12:1-3; 26:3-4; 28:13-14; 49:10; 2 Sam. 7:11-16).

Before David died, he proclaimed his son Solomon king. God appeared to the young king Solomon and told him to ask what he would. Solomon asked for wisdom. God was pleased and granted him wisdom far above others. In addition, God gave him riches, honor, peace, and long life, if he lived

faithfully. Solomon did build the temple as God had promised. The fame of his wisdom and wealth spread abroad. He wrote Proverbs, Ecclesiastes, and Song of Solomon. The nation of Israel reached its greatest size during his reign. Unfortunately, he was led away from God by his many wives.

THE KINGDOM DIVIDES

The kingdom was in distress by the time Solomon died. He had overburdened the people with taxes and they wanted relief. When Rehoboam his son became king, the ten northern tribes rebelled because Rehoboam would not listen to their pleas for relief. Jeroboam became king over the northern portion of the land, which retained the name Israel, as the nation had always been called. Rehoboam was left with only two tribes in the south, and he called his little kingdom Judah.

The history of the Israelite nation had ended another phase. Israel left Egypt as a vast multitude of untrained slaves. God molded, taught, and reshaped the nation during the forty years of wilderness wandering under Moses. Joshua led an enthusiastic, conquering nation into Canaan, the promised land. Then followed the period of judges when each man "did that which was right in his own eyes" (Judg. 21:25). The people wanted a king and worked together under Saul, David, and Solomon during the period called the United Kingdom. Now the kingdom has divided into two small, sometimes warring, kingdoms. From this point through the rest of the Old Testament, the people fall farther and farther away from God.

Jeroboam of the northern kingdom did not want his subjects returning to the temple at Jerusalem. He established his own system of worship: new gods, new priests, new feast days, new laws. There was never a righteous king in Israel. The dynasty changed nine times before the kingdom fell! Ahab, with his wicked wife Jezebel, stands out as one of the most wicked kings of the period. Elijah, Elisha, Amos, Hosea, and other prophets were sent by God to warn Israel of impending doom. Again space does not permit us to go into detail. Finally, God would tolerate their wickedness no longer. In 721 BC God allowed the Assyrian army to overthrow Samaria, the capital of Israel. The people were led away captives, and foreigners were brought in to fill the land. These foreigners intermarried with the low class Israelites left in the land and became the hated mixed race later called the Samaritans.

After this, the southern kingdom of Judah continued, but they, too, drifted away from God. Their descent downward was not as fast as Israel's, however, because they did have some good kings such as Asa, Jehoshaphat, Uzziah, Hezekiah, and Josiah. There is no darker period in Israelite history than the divided kingdom. Finally, God's patience was exhausted with Judah also (2 Chron. 36:15-16). In 606 BC Nebuchadnezzar of Babylon led the first captives away from Jerusalem. He returned for more captives in 597 BC, and finally destroyed the city of Jerusalem in 586 BC Only the poorest of the land were left, and even they fled to Egypt within a few months.

THE NORTHERN KINGDOM FALLS TO ASSYRIA, JUDAH IS LEFT ALONE

JUDAH FALLS TO BABYLON. JEWS CARRIED AWAY INTO EXILE.

Has God forgotten His plan? Is it all over? Never for one moment! God's chosen people must be punished, but He did not allow man's weaknesses to destroy His eternal purpose.

Do you remember the promise to David that the royal line would remain in his family (2 Sam. 7:11-16)? The ruling family changed nine times in Israel, but never once in Judah. God's providence supplied a direct descendant in each generation. On one occasion, Athaliah the daughter of Ahab tried to destroy all the royal seed and usurp the throne (2 Kings 11:1-4). The baby Joash was hidden by Jehoida the priest for six years before he was brought to the throne. Another time, an enemy destroyed all the royal line, except for one son (2 Chron. 21:16-17). It was no accident that one was left each time to take his place on David's throne. These kings were important links in the plan of God.

The same passage that promised the royal line would remain in David's family also warned that his descendants would be punished if they were wicked. The punishment that came to the house of Judah was as much a part of God's plan as the blessings they could have had if they had remained faithful.

The writings of the prophets Daniel and Ezekiel tell of the captivity. Trained to serve in the court of the kings, Daniel held positions of high authority under Nebuchadnezzar, and then under Darius of the Medes and Persians. Ezekiel lived among the common people and gives us an insight into their lives during the period.

Jeremiah the prophet had foretold the captivity would last for seventy years (Jer. 25:11). Sure enough, the first captives had been taken in 606 BC In 539 BC, Babylon fell to the Medes and Persians. King Cyrus decreed that all captive people might return to their original homes. Thus, in 536 BC, exactly seventy years after the first captives had been taken from Judah, a group of Jews started for their homeland. Zerubbabel led this first group. Their main objective was to rebuild the temple in Jerusalem.

As is usual in any worthwhile task, the people immediately faced opposition. The neighboring Samaritans interfered, and finally succeeded in stopping the work on the temple. For sixteen years nothing was done. The

THE RETURN

prophets Haggai and Zechariah urged the people to resume their work. The temple was finally completed, but the people did not remain faithful to God.

Ezra brought another group back to Jerusalem and set about to restore the worship of the people (458 BC). Not much later, Nehemiah learned that the city was still in distress. He received permission from the king of Persia to rebuild the walls of Jerusalem. He and the people worked hard and completed the huge task in only 52 days. Nehemiah and Ezra worked together to persuade the people to put away their foreign wives and to return to faithfulness to God.

The percentage of Jews who returned to their native land was actually small. By this time there were Jews scattered all over the then known world. God did not forget His people wherever they were living. The book of Esther shows how God could exert His providence even in the court of a Persian king in order to save His people.

The prophet Amos had predicted that a day of famine would come, not of food or water, but rather a famine of hearing the words of the Lord (Amos 8:11). That time came following Malachi, who prophesied in the days of Nehemiah and Ezra.

We get our clearest picture of the spiritual condition of the people during this period from Malachi's writings. They went through a form of worship, but their hearts were not in it. Malachi closes his book by saying there would come one in the style of Elijah to prepare the way "before the coming of the great and dreadful day of the Lord" (Mal. 4:5).

The prophets had foretold additional information about this special One who was to come, but He was still a shadowy figure at this point.

THE YEARS OF SILENCE

Now complete silence. The curtain has fallen upon the divine stage, and four hundred years pass with no recorded communication from God. Has He changed His mind? Has His purpose been forgotten?

Babylon fell before the Old Testament closed. The Medo-Persian Empire fell about one hundred years after Malachi's book was written. Alexander the Great led the Greeks as they conquered the world. Years passed, and Rome, the fourth world empire since Daniel's day, rose to power. God's prophecy had been that in the days of this empire He would establish His kingdom which would never be destroyed (Dan. 2:44). "The fullness of the times" had come (see Gal. 4:4).

The curtain rises again to find an old priest named Zacharias serving in the temple. Suddenly, the angel Gabriel stood before him—the first communication from God since Malachi. Zacharias received the news that he was to be the father of John, the forerunner who was predicted by Malachi.

THE BIRTH OF JESUS

Some six months later the same angel appeared to a young virgin named Mary. He told her she would have a child, conceived of the Holy Spirit. This would be Jesus, the Savior; Immanuel, God with us; Christ, the Anointed One; the Word become flesh to dwell among men.

It is this One—the Divine Son of God—who had come to sum up all the glorious plan of God. He is the One who fulfills the promises and prophecies. He is the One who offered the sacrifice of death for sin so that man might live in spite of his weaknesses. He is the One who gave the perfect law of liberty that man might live a new life filled with hope. He is the One who is the fullness of the whole Bible. There would be no Bible, no plan, no hope for man without this Jesus.

Matthew, Mark, Luke, and John were written that we might understand and believe that this Jesus fits every qualification ever set by God to be the Messiah. He was indeed the "Christ, the Son of the Living

God." He lived a perfect life to show man the life that is in God. He died to pay the price for sin and was raised to be the firstfruits of them that sleep. He was crowned in heaven itself to reign on David's throne at the right hand of God.

GO TELL THE GOOD NEWS

Just before Jesus went back to heaven, He told His disciples to "go ye into all the world, and preach the gospel to every creature" (Mark 16:15). The word gospel literally means "good news." In other words, Jesus was telling His disciples to go spread the good news. Go tell the world that the Promised One has come. Go tell every person there is hope for forgiveness, there is hope for a home in heaven. Go tell the world that man may be reconciled with God. Go tell the world that God's plan for redemption has been revealed.

The apostles were given the Holy Spirit to guide them as they went throughout the world to tell people of this glorious plan of God. The book of Acts gives us a glimpse of the type work that was done.

By the end of the first century, the new law, the law of Christ, had been fully revealed and written for mankind to read, understand, and

THE PERFECT LAW OF LIBERTY

accept (Eph. 3:1-12). Laws and rules were given to guide us in shaping our lives to be like Christ, to partake of the divine nature (2 Pet. 1:4).

The prophets of the Old Testament wanted to see the end of the picture (1 Pet. 1:10-12). We have it all revealed now in Christ. People of this era are heirs of the promises made to Abraham, Isaac, and Jacob (Acts 3:24-25). There is no other spiritual blessing we could ask.

The glorious, eternal plan of God is ready for us to accept. It is our choice. We may accept its terms and inherit the blessings, or we may reject its terms and be lost and without hope in the world. Life on earth is a short trial period to see which men may live in heaven with God for eternity.

The New Testament closes with a book of victory. Revelation foretells the final victory of Christ over Satan at the judgment day.

The entire Bible is the story of Christ, the fullness of the scheme of redemption!

Yes, I *must* accept God's terms. I must believe His word. I must repent of my sins, I must confess His name before men, and I must be baptized to become a child of God. Then, I must live the rest of my life imitating the nature of Christ to the best of my ability. But would it not be more appropriate to say *I am given the privilege to meet God's terms?*

(The preceding summary of the Bible is taken from a tract we have written called "The Unfolding of God's Plan, The Story of The Scheme of Redemption," and from the fourth chapter of our teachers' training book called *A Generation That Knows Not God,* pp. 27-39.)

The Bible Story Is Our Curriculum

Too many argue there is no reason to study the whole Bible. We do not live under the law of Moses, so why bother to learn about it?

It is true that the law God gave at Mount Sinai was given only to the Jews, and was taken out of effect for them when the new law of Christ was set in order. It is true that we were never told to build an ark to escape a flood, nor were we told to go warn the people of Nineveh that their city would be destroyed within forty days if they did not repent. It is true that when I reach the judgment throne of God I will be judged by how well I served under the law of Christ.

But how can I understand the law of Christ? How can I understand the blessing of forgiveness? How can I understand the language of redemption? It is the Old Testament that tells how sin entered the world in the first place. It teaches the concept of a sacrifice being offered whereby another can be saved. It shows how God makes promises of blessings for those who serve Him and promises of punishment for those who disobey Him—then it shows how God keeps every one of those promises. The Old Testament shows God to be a God of justice and righteousness, but also to be a God of love and mercy. How can I fully understand the nature of God without the history of how He has treated mankind?

The summary of the Bible story shows how beautifully it all fits together. Neither testament is complete without the other. Suppose there had never been a Christ; suppose there had never been a New Testament. Then all the promises of the Old Testament concerning this One to bless all nations would have been left dangling.

But what if there had never been an Old Testament? Try to imagine a copy of the New Testament with all references to the Old Testament cut out. You would not be able to find one whole page throughout the entire volume. We would be horrified to see someone mutilate a Bible in this way; yet we accomplish the same thing when we refuse to study the Old Testament. We leave great holes in our understanding of the New Testament. The Old Testament is the very foundation upon which the New Testament is laid.

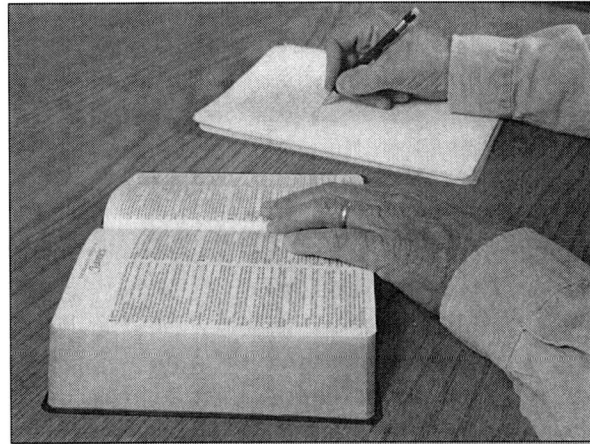

The Old Testament without the New would be no more complete than a house without a roof. But the New Testament without the Old would be no more complete than a house without a foundation. Each is incomplete without the other.

One of the most serious things wrong with the attitude that we do not need to teach the Old Testament is that we thereby condemn Jesus and the apostles because they made extensive use of the Old Testament. They used it to make their arguments and to illustrate their points. Let us beware, lest in our blindness, we take a position which condemns what they did.

God in His wisdom gave us a book containing 66 smaller books. How can I, as a puny human being, lift my face to heaven and say, "I do not need all this book You gave. I'll pick and choose the parts I want"? Put into words like that, it sounds almost like blasphemy, does it not? Instead, with humility, I need to submit my puny wisdom to His wisdom and learn the lessons He felt were important for me to learn. "*All scripture is given by the inspiration of God and is profitable...*" (2 Tim. 3:16).

Purpose for These Books

Through the years, most of our classes have failed to convey a coherent grasp of the whole Bible. We have tended to follow the same time-worn methods year in and year out, methods which obviously do not get the task done. We have gone through the motions of teaching without any real learning taking place. It is possible for us to know our Bibles, and for our children to know theirs. All it takes is a common sense approach to the matter, and confidence that it can be done. Just remember that every class, every chart, every flannel-graph story, every visual aid, must be directed to teaching the Bible in a coherent manner.

Obviously, one class period is not long enough to tell the details of the entire Bible story. Today's lesson may zero in on the story of David and the giant, which is a story children love. But in order for the story to serve the purpose God intended, it should follow last week's story of the rejection of Saul's kingdom and the anointing of the young man David. Next week's lesson should pick up where we stopped with the story of the giant and tell how Saul grew jealous. Even tiny tots can learn the sequence of the Bible story. This is the God-given heritage our children deserve. *This story is what we must teach our children.* If you do not know the story, it is time to learn it. Waiting another day is postponing it too long.

This study of Genesis is the first of a series of books covering the Bible narrative. These books are not workbooks, nor are they commentaries. They are more, however, than mere study guides. They fill a much needed spot because most people either do not own commentaries or they have trouble understanding them. Our belief is that most of the Bible does not need extensive explanation. In an effort to keep this material simple, we do not include many references to scholarly works.

We have tried to avoid, as much as possible, long, technical notes.

This book and those that follow were written because present teaching methods have been so poor, many teachers who were trying hard to use the Bible as their curriculum were having great difficulty taking the Bible text and putting the stories into their own words. We have, therefore, "retold" the stories in more common language and have included just enough notes to clarify the narrative. There are many places where we were aware of problems where fuller notes could have been given, but we felt that doing so would have been inappropriate in a study on this level and for our purposes.

The series of books is designed for a survey study of the entire Bible. In the classes where they have been used as the foundation of the curriculum, the classes have been set up to study the same course on Sunday morning and Wednesday night, and move as quickly as possible through the narrative. Thus, in one quarter, the stories of Genesis can be studied and learned. Using this pattern, the entire Bible can be surveyed in three or four years. Of course, there are advantages and disadvantages in a survey course in contrast to a detailed study. If you only survey, then there is never time to learn the minute details; but if you only look at details, such as the detailed meaning of each word, then you never learn the overall picture. These books would help with either type study, but they were designed for the survey because we feel that is the area that has been most neglected in our classes.

The material is not designed for you to read it aloud to your students. In fact, to be effective, do not read either the Bible text or this book aloud to your class. Instead, study your text thoroughly, read this material to help you better understand exactly what was happening, and then present the information in such a way you make the story "come alive."

These books will be a great help to anyone from junior high and up to understand the Bible better, but they are designed to help teachers. Therefore, throughout, there are suggestions made about teaching the material. Use the books freely with those who have never taught classes before. This series can help untaught Christians become well-taught teachers, ready to help others grow in their knowledge.

Study maps and blank maps are included in the books where they are needed. Permission is freely given to copy these maps for use with classes. Our only request about the maps is that you do not market the maps you have copied.

We also encourage every teacher to have copies of our other books: *The History and Geography of the Bible Story* and *A Generation That Knows Not God* (a manual with suggestions on how to teach the Bible). The geography book will help the teacher gain a grasp of the overall Bible story with a fuller understanding of where each event happened. The teacher's book will help the teacher gain a grasp of the overall Bible story with a fuller understanding of where each event happened. The teacher's book will help the teacher gain insight into how students of various ages learn best, and what is fair to expect each age to learn.

Introduction to Genesis

Look at the periods of Bible history in your right column. Memorize these periods because they will serve as the skeleton for this whole series of studies about the scheme of redemption.

The book of Genesis covers four periods of Bible history: the Creation, the Flood, the Scattering of the People, and the Patriarchs. We have made these four groups of stories into major headings of our outline. Though the chapters covered are very few in comparison to the other periods, the length of time these periods cover is very great. Genesis forms the foundation of the rest of the Bible.

The book of Genesis is in a group with the four following books: Exodus, Leviticus, Numbers, and Deuteronomy. These five books are called the Pentateuch *(Pente=five; teuchos=book)*. The Jews called these books the Torah. Not only does this section of the Bible contain the commandments of the law of Moses, but in a larger sense, the whole section exemplifies the principles on the basis of which God deals with men. The Torah seeks to instill these principles into the hearts of those who read it. As we teach the Torah, we need to follow its plan. Therefore we will *tell* the narrative material and *expound* the expository sections. Genesis definitely belongs to the narrative material.

The earliest portion of the Pentateuch written was probably Exodus 20-23 (see Exod. 24:4). Genesis was written during the forty years between the time the Israelites left Egypt and entered Canaan, along with the other books of the Pentateuch.

The book of Genesis was written by Moses, as he was guided by the Holy Spirit. In textual criticism, as in everything else, liberalism has made its biased presence known. In the latter part of the nineteenth century, the Graf-Wellhausen theory, also known as the Documentary Hypothesis, denied that Moses wrote the books of the Pentateuch. Let us look at some of the arguments the theory makes and give some of the answers:

- One of the major pillars on which the theory was based was that writing was unknown in the days of Moses (c. 1450 BC).

- **Creation**
- **The Flood**
- **Scattering of People**
- **The Patriarchs**

The Exodus
Wandering
Conquest of Land
Judges
United Kingdom
Divided Kingdom
Judah Alone
Captivity
Return
Years of Silence
Life of Christ
Early Church
Letters to Christians

- It has now been well established that writing *was known* long before Moses. For example, more than 100,000 clay tablets found at Nuzi date back to the second millennium BC (1700-2000 BC). But the discovery that writing was common in the days of Moses has not changed the liberal view of the authorship of the Pentateuch.

- Scholars who deny Mosaic authorship have a problem explaining why there are more archaic words in the Pentateuch than in any other section of the Bible.
  - The most obvious reason for these archaic words is that the Pentateuch was written earliest.
  - Another reason for believing in the antiquity of the Pentateuch is that the social customs and history recorded in it reflect the environment of the day.
  - Similarly, the nature of the covenant between God and Israel reflects typical vassal treaties of the day when the Pentateuch claims to have been written.
  - Therefore, both the internal evidence of the language itself and the customs mentioned support the authorship of Moses.

- The Documentary Hypothesis says that the Pentateuch was composed from a collection of writings by different authors. The theory is based to a great extent upon the different styles of writing which liberal scholars think they find in these books.
  - If these same, rather arbitrary, methods were used on other works of literature, they could show that there were several writers who wrote *War and Peace* or *Torn Sawyer*, or any other book.

- One argument for different authors is that there are different words used to apply to God. For example, in Genesis 2:4-3:24, the name Jehovah God (*Yahweh Elohim*) is found again and again. Skeptics use this variation from 1:1-2:3, where *Elohim* is used, along with other variations found in the book, to say Genesis was put together from the writings of various unknown men.

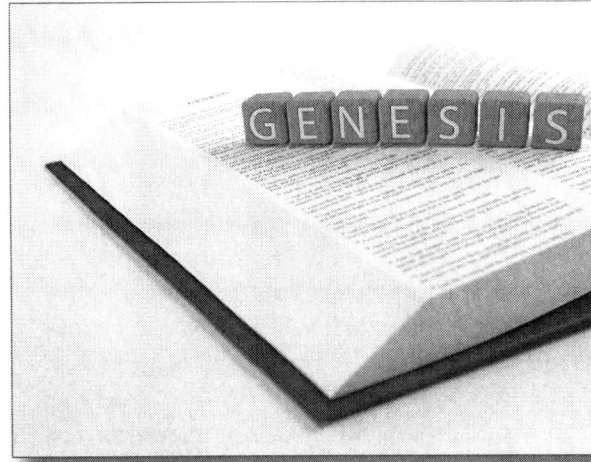

- But the best explanation for the variations is that each name used for God is declaring some particular aspect of His nature. A given name was used in a particular context in order to make a specific point about what God was doing at that time.

We therefore have no reason whatever to reject Moses as the author of the Pentateuch, including the book of Genesis. The attempt to reject his authorship contradicts plain Bible statements that he did write it. (See Exod. 24:4; 34:27; Num. 33:2; Deut. 31:9; Josh. 8:32; Mark 10:4-5; 12:19; John 1:45.) We will proceed on the premise that Genesis and the rest of the Pentateuch is exactly what it claims to be—the inspired record of the history of man from the very beginning, and the account of God's dealings with early men.

How can we choose to believe that Jesus died for our sins, and that we have a hope of heaven, and at the same time deny that the first chapter of the Bible is true? How could we know which parts to believe and which to disbelieve? Perhaps an even more basic question is: If God did not create us, then what right does He have to command us? If God has no right to give us commands, then what right does any being have to command us? If no one can command us, then my rights, my ideas are supreme—and your rights and ideas are supreme—and we have total anarchy. There can be no order in society. The entire Bible stands or falls as a unit. It is all God's word and must be taken as such.

Study the Outline of Genesis

The brief outline below shows that Genesis is divided into two main sections. The first section covers chapters 1-11, the second chapters 12-50. The first section contains three groups of stories: The creation stories, the flood, and the scattering of the people, with the specific story of the Tower of Babel. The second section falls into portions as we follow the lives of four men: Abraham, Isaac, Jacob, and Joseph. Memorize this short outline.

In the detailed outline, notice that we list each of the main stories in the first section under separate headings—not because they cover many chapters in the Bible, but because they cover many years. During this earliest period of all, God included only the information that was of universal importance. We are told very little about the people who lived during those years.

Then, in the second section, we group the stories about all four men under the heading called the Patriarchs. The word "Patriarch" means "father-ruler." Abraham, Isaac, and Jacob are the ones who were the fathers of the Israelite nation, so they are the ones that would technically fit under the heading of Patriarchs, but since thirteen of the last fourteen chapters of Genesis tell the story of Joseph, no outline of the book would be complete without listing his story under a distinct heading.

As you proceed with the study of Genesis, look back frequently to the outline to get a feel for the flow of events. It is an easy book to learn. Too often we expect too little of ourselves, and we will study a book over and over without ever actually learning it. Take this opportunity to learn the stories of Genesis thoroughly, using the outlines (both the short one and the detailed one) to get the overview in mind and then the text itself to get the details in mind.

I. First section—chapters 1-11
    A. Before the flood—chapters 1-5
        1. Creation of the world—chapters 1-2
        2. First sin—chapter 3
        3. Cain and Abel—chapter 4
        4. Generations of Adam—chapter 5
    B. The flood—chapters 6-9
    C. The scattering of the people - chapters 10-11
        1. Generations of the sons of Noah—chapter 10
        2. The Tower of Babel—11:1-9
        3. The generations of Shem—11:10-32

II. Second section—chapters 12-50
    A. Abraham—12:1-25:18
    B. Isaac—25:19-28:9; 35:27-29
    C. Jacob—28:10-36:43; 38
    D. Joseph—37:1-36; 39:1-50:26

The Creation Stories
(Genesis 1:1-5:32)

Creation of the Heavens and the Earth
(Genesis 1:1-2:25)

Day One (1:1-5):

Once there was nothing but God. At some point in the existence of God, He created the heavens and the earth. By His command the far flung universe came into being. He stretched out the heavens like a curtain (Psa. 104:2).

At first the earth was completely uninhabitable; its entire surface was covered by water, and darkness was everywhere. The Spirit of God, however, hovered above the earth, as a mother bird over her nest, contemplating the mighty acts which He was about to perform.

Then God said: "Light, be!" And light suddenly shined in the darkness. There was evening of the first creation day followed by morning—day one.

The book of Genesis is not a book of natural history, nor a scientific treatise. Neither is it written to gratify curiosity. It merely sets forth that God made the heavens and the earth by His own power.

There is not the slightest evidence that there was a gap between verse one and verse two. The efforts of men to uphold the unproven theory of evolution cause them to seek to force the Bible into a mold of their own making. Regardless of the claims of evolution, there is no basis in the language of Genesis for a gap between the verses. The conjunction translated "and" at the beginning of verse 2 is used to continue a narrative, implying there was no gap. Nowhere in the Bible is there the slightest evidence of such a gap.

The reason why the "gap theory" was thought of was to give an opportunity for a Pre-Adamic world to exist, in which there were dinosaurs and perhaps other life forms. According to the theory, these creatures all died out in that world, and their fossils were left. Such a theory is not only unnecessary, it is riddled with problems. It raises more questions than it answers. This world would have existed before light, or else light was created twice. It was a world without the sun or moon to make the seasons and years. When this world ceased, not the slightest vestige of it was left, not even vegetation, because God had to create even the grass on the third day. This theory would require that dinosaurs fossils always be found on the bottom-most layers of the strata of rocks; but that is not the case.

The chief reason why the gap theory cannot be maintained is that Moses said that in six days God made heaven and earth, the sea, and all that in them is (Exod. 20:11). The gap theory excludes the heavens and the earth from the six days of creation. According to it, the heavens and the earth were created, followed by an age or ages, then the six creation days. Moses says the creation of the heavens and earth was included within the six days.

Let no Bible teacher set out to affirm a theory at which the Bible does not remotely hint. Certainly let no one be moved to do so by the unproven theory of evolution. There is so much speculation and guesswork among the supporters of evolution that we should never begin rearranging the Bible each time they come up with their latest decrees.

Day Two (1:6-8):

On the second day God created a firmament, a space or expanse between the waters upon the earth and the waters above the earth. He called this expanse heaven. That is, He made the space in which we live and move, that we call air, and He made what we call the sky where the clouds are. There was evening followed by another morning—day two.

Since the Bible is not a scientific book, and makes no effort to be one, we must not try to make it into a scientific treatise. To people who did not know about vaporization, condensation, relative humidity, and dew points, it would appear that rain came from vaults in the sky. Some say that the Hebrews thought the firmament was solid, yet early man knew that rainfall was associated with clouds, so we should be cautious in attributing levels of knowledge or ignorance to them.

From a practical standpoint, the creation of the firmament meant that, normally, men would not live in a cloud of fog, but that the clouds would float above the earth. The word "heavens" in verse one includes the universe with its galaxies, stars, and planets. The word "heaven" in verse 8 is the earth's sky. The whole Bible uses the word "heaven" in three different senses: the two ways we find it here, plus heaven as the abode of God.

Day Three (1:9-13):

Then God said, "Let the waters upon the earth be gathered into one place and let the dry land appear." Continents and mountains rose out of the seas while millions of tons of water cascaded from their shoulders to form oceans.

Once the dry land was exposed, God commanded that the earth bring forth grasses, in which the seed are very tiny and not even in evidence at times. He called for the herbaceous plants, producing seed which would include all vegetable plants, and for fruit trees bearing fruit after their kind. So the earth put forth these three categories of plants, each bearing seed after its kind, and God saw that it was good. This day was the third.

By one enormous act, the surface of the earth was given the appearance of great age. What a mountain-building process would require millions of years to do, God accomplished in a moment by His command and by the exercise of His will, as land appeared from the seas. The forces presently at work upon the earth's crust were created when the earth was made, but the earth's surface cannot be explained by the uniform, uninterrupted operation of these

forces. The creation of the seas, and the rising of the continents, plus the flood of Noah's day, greatly accelerated the various aspects of those forces affecting the earth's crust.

By God's commands the earth was covered with grasses, vegetables, and trees. The creation was miraculous. God did not merely begin life, He created it full grown. Thus there would have been trees on the third day appearing to be grown. The appearance of age was not an effort by God to deceive—rather it was the result of the miraculous creation of a world ready to be inhabited.

It is argued by many who are eager to reconcile the demands of evolution with the Bible that these days were great ages. But note these facts:

- For ages to be any help to evolutionists, they must be not merely a thousand years long, but many millions of years long.

- One would never derive the idea of day/ages from reading the text.

- Throughout the rest of the Old Testament, the Hebrew word for day (yom) invariably means a twenty-four hour day when used in conjunction with a numeral such as first, second, etc.

- The terms "evening and morning" point to a twenty-four hour day.

- What would the evenings be in a period of millions of years? If it refers to the period of dark-

ness as it does everywhere else in the Scriptures, then there would have been some hundreds of thousands of years (or even millions of years) for plants to be in darkness. Thus not only would an unusual meaning have to be given to "day," but also to "evening."

- The account of Moses says that, In six days Jehovah made heaven and earth, the sea, and all that in them is, and rested the seventh day: wherefore Jehovah blessed the sabbath day, and hallowed it" (Exod 20:11). The seventh day here is a twenty-four hour day because it is used to show why God chose Saturday as the day of rest for the Israelites. In the context the term "six days" would mean six twenty-four hour days.

- If one chooses the theory of evolution over the account of the creation told in Genesis 1, he has to deny many more passages than that one chapter. The Bible affirms the creation over and over again (see Exod. 20:11; Psa. 104.4 9; Isa. 42:5; Acts 14:15; 17:24).

Again let me remind you that you must not seek to accommodate the Bible to theories of men which come and go. Teach the creation as the Bible says and let the theories of men contend for themselves. It is beyond the scope of this study to go into detail on the subject of evolution, yet all of us, especially our young people in school, are barraged with evolutionist propaganda on every side, and we need help in learning how to counteract what we hear. Our young people need help to see that the theories they are hearing at school or on television are in direct conflict with the Bible text. Sometimes they hear both accounts, and do not understand how much they contradict each other. You may need to read some of the good works that are available dealing with evolution. See the bibliography for a list of some good books on the subject.

Day Four (1:14-19):

On the fourth day God said, "Let there be lights in the face of the sky to divide the day from the night. Let them be also for signs, for seasons, and for days and years."

Therefore God made two great lights: the greater light to govern the day and the lesser light to rule the night. He made the stars also. God set these lights in the heavens to give light to the earth, to govern the day and the night, and to divide the light from the darkness, and He was pleased.

There was light in existence from verse 3, day one. There was darkness and light from that first day forward Yet the sun and moon are not mentioned until day four. How is that explained? We cannot do away with evening and morning from the three days preceding day four without erasing the words from the text. Therefore, God was making a separation between day and night, light and darkness, from the first day. That He did not need the sun and moon to do this should be apparent to anyone who believes in the power of a God capable of doing all these things. It was obviously God's plan that the earth be subject to an alternating pattern of darkness and light. He began this pattern on day one with the creation of light. The most obvious explanation is that He maintained this pattern until day four by His special power and then ordained a natural arrangement whereby the same results would be accomplished.

The sun and moon may well have been created as a part of the heavens and the earth from the beginning (1:1). Just as God worked organizing and finishing the earth, so He finished and organized the heavens. Therefore, on this fourth day, God may have set in order the precise rotations of each body in the solar system, as we know it today. Since the text does not specify exactly what God did, or how He did it, it is useless for us to speculate further.

It does not make sense that the sun and moon were already doing their appointed tasks on days one, two, and three. If they had, they would have been doing well for three days what the Bible says God set them doing on the fourth day. Therefore, our explanation agrees with the text better than other explanations.

Day Five (1:20-23):

On the fifth day God commanded, "Let the waters teem with schools of creatures, and let birds fly above the earth in the sky." So God created the great sea creatures *(literally the "stretched out creatures," the great fish and whales)* and all the teeming schools of creatures in the sea after their kind, and all the birds that fly after their kind.

God blessed them and said, "Be fruitful, and multiply, and fill the waters of the seas, and let the birds multiply on the earth."

Day Six (1:24-31):

God said, "Let the earth produce living creatures after their kind, cattle, creeping things *(animals with no legs or with very small legs)*, and the freely moving animals of the earth *(carnivores and swift moving herds of animals such as antelopes)*." When the animals were created, God was pleased.

There is a very clear distinction between the way God created the land animals and the way He created man. Notice the distinction as we continue to study the passage.

But the creation was not yet complete. God said, "Let us make man in our own image, after our likeness, and let them rule over the fish of the sea, over the birds of the heavens, over the cattle, and over all the earth." So God made man in His own image and created him male and female. God blessed them and said, "Be fruitful, and multiply, and fill the earth and subdue it, and have dominion over all its creatures."

He continued, "Look, I have given you the herbaceous vegetables and the fruit trees for food. This same food will be for every beast of the earth, to the birds, and to the creeping things."

There was evening and there was morning, day six.

When God said, "Let us" (1:26), to whom did He speak? The term God in this first chapter is the word "Elohim" which is plural in form. It is used frequently in the Bible to refer to the Godhead; it is used of angels (Psa. 8:5; Heb. 2:7); it is used of false gods, of which there are many; and on at least one occasion, it is used of the judges and magistrates of Israel who administered the law of God (Psalm 82; see also Exod. 22:28).

Some suggest that "us" is the majestic plural, in the same sense in which a king says "we" and "us" even when he includes no one but himself.

We must reject the explanation that God was speaking to the angels, because men are not made in the image of angels, but of God (Acts 17:28-29). Whoever the "us" is, it includes all that is God, all that is divine (Gen. 1:27).

The explanation is provided by the subsequent revelation of God's threefold existence in the Father, the Son, and the Holy Spirit. All three are God— Deity— and all three were involved in creation. (See Job 26:13; John 1:3.) In other words, there are three Divine Beings that compose God—thus the plural term Elohim even though it is referring to the one Godhead.

The image of God and His likeness are synonymous. They refer to the spiritual essence of God. Man,

of all the creatures, possesses that spiritual essence, a soul. God equipped man with a high degree of intelligence, a will, consciousness, a soul—all the things that make man different from all other creatures. They are also the characteristics that enable man to worship God Human beings are not automatically like God in life and character, but God made them with the <u>capacity</u> to be like Him. How sad when men waste their gifts and live like mere animals.

What is included in the dominion given unto men? Man was given the ability to turn the world to his own use, to use its products as he saw fit. Men in general have not been able to exercise complete dominion over the creation, but of one of their number, Jesus the Christ, it is said that all things have been put in subjection under His feet (Eph. 1:21-22; 1 Cor. 15:27; Heb. 2:5-8). In Him this promise is ultimately fulfilled.

Notice that plants were given for food at this point, not animals. Human beings, animals, and birds all ate plants at this time. Watch for meat to be added to the diet later.

Memorize the Creation Days:

Day One—Light
Day Two—Firmament
Day Three—Dry land, plants
Day Four—Sun, moon, stars
Day Five—Fish, birds
Day Six—Animals, man
Day Seven—God rested

Day Seven (2:1-3):

Thus the heavens and the earth were finished, and all the things in them. On the seventh day God was finished with His work which He had done, and He rested on that day. God blessed the seventh day and set it apart because on it He ceased from the work which He had created.

God did not rest because He was tired. On that seventh day He continued working: holding the whole universe together, including the earth, and upholding all the laws of nature (see Col. 1:17). The point is that there was no further creative act. The work was complete.

The book of Genesis was written by Moses, probably after the episodes at Mount Sinai that are recorded in Exodus. This note about God blessing the seventh day was probably recorded, therefore, after the sabbath law was given (Exod 20:8-11). Nehemiah said that God made known His holy sabbath by Moses (Neh. 9:14). Moses said that God gave the sabbath to Israel because they had been slaves in Egypt (Deut. 5:15). To have a day of rest would remind them that they were free, and it would be a continual token of God's mercy. The seventh day was the one chosen and hallowed by God as the sabbath because it was the day when He ceased His creative work (Exod. 20:11). But even though it says here in Genesis 2:3 that God sancti-fied the day, there is no mention at all of anyone being told to observe the day in any way until the Israelites were told to keep it in Exodus 16:5, 22-26. In even that first passage about the sabbath, the full law was not given about their day of rest. The law was given as part of the ten commandments as God spoke from Mount Sinai (Exod 20:11), and then was expanded and fully explained as the rest of the law was given through Moses. The new law, the Law of Christ, does not include laws concerning a sab-bath, a day of rest. Under the new law, we observe the first day of the week with its obligations, rather than the seventh day of the week, because it was upon the first day of the week that our Savior arose from the dead

The Garden of Eden (2:4-17):

God is called Elohim from Genesis 1:1 through 2:3, and then the expression changes to Jehovah God (Yahweh Elohim) from 2:4 through 3:24. God is emphasizing that Elohim the Creator is also the God who manifests Himself to man and deals with man in a personal way. The word Jehovah is devel-oped from the Hebrew imperfect of the verb lo be. "Jehovah is the "manifested One, the One who shows Himself to man throughout history. The combination of the two names shows that Jehovah, who manifests Himself from time to time in the affairs of men, is also the eternal God who made the heavens and the

The Euphrates River in modern Iraq.

earth. That is: Elohim, the God of eternity, is also Jehovah, the God of time and history. This refutes any theory that indicates God, or some Supreme Be-ing, created the earth and life, and then left it to its own devices.

The events in chapter two are the further developments of the heavens and the earth at the time they were created by Jehovah God. No plant or herb of the field had yet grown, because Jehovah God had not caused it to rain upon the earth, and there was not a man to till the ground. But a mist went up from the earth and watered the whole face of the ground; and Jehovah God formed man from the dust of the ground and breathed into his nostrils the breath of life, and man became a living being.

Jehovah God planted a garden eastward in Eden, and there He placed man. God caused all sorts of trees to grow there—beautiful trees, and trees that were good for food. The Tree of Life was in the midst of the garden and also the Tree of Knowledge of Good and Evil. A river went out of Eden to water the garden. After that, it divided into four heads: the Pishon, the Gihon, the Hiddekel, and the Euphrates.

God placed man in the garden and told him to dress and keep it. He said to the man, "You may freely eat of every tree in the garden, except for one. Do not eat of the Tree of the Knowledge of

Good and Evil, because in the day you eat of it you will certainly die."

When did the events of chapter 2 take place? God created the vegetation on the third day, and it existed from that point forward. Yet in chapter 2 we are at a point where no vegetation is growing because there has been no rain and there is not a man to till the soil. But man was not created until the sixth day. Was there no vegetation until the sixth day, until finally there was a man to till the soil? One explanation is that this chapter is giving more details about day three and day six when plants and man were created. But that raises some difficulties. It may mean that there were plants from the third day forward, but the processes necessary to make them sprout and grow had not been fully finished The creation of vegetation did not depend upon rain and cultivation, but the sprouting and growing of plants and seed would

Perhaps a better explanation is that the reference here is to the preparation of the Garden of Eden. The verse mentions only 'the plant of the field and the herb of the field" (2:5), and that does not embrace the variety of the grasses, herbaceous vegetables, and fruit trees created on the third day (1:11-12). The term "field" is not the globe, but a "portion of land fit for cultivation."

Note that there are two reasons given why the plants and herbs had not yet sprung up. In 2:6 the first problem is solved: it rained; God set in order the laws of condensation, evaporation, and rain. Then in 2:7, the second obstacle to plant growth was overcome: man was formed.

The rivers Pishon and Gihon cannot be identified with any certainty. The land of Havilah is probably not the Arabian Havilah that later existed, since the products associated with Havilah in this passage are not those customarily associated with Arabian Havilah. Cush, here associated with the Gihon, is probably a region called in the Greek, "Cossaia," in the area between the Black Sea and the Caspian Sea, but no one knows for sure. The Hiddekel is without doubt the Tigris River (see Dan. 10:4),

and the Euphrates continued to be known by that same name.

The facts given point to a location for the Garden of Eden in northern Mesopotamia, although the land forms have changed somewhat since those long-gone days, because there is now no single river which breaks into these four rivers. But Moses' use of the names of two rivers which were well known to the people of his day argues that these rivers were in the same approximate location before the flood that they were afterwards.

The Tree of Life was a unique blessing in the garden. By eating of its fruit one could have indefinite life. On the other hand, the Tree of Knowledge of Good and Evil was given as a test of man's faith and of his willingness to obey God. The knowledge of good and evil would come from the act of disobedience, not from some ingredient found in the fruit. God did not want men to serve Him merely because there was no choice. This commandment gave man the choice to love God or to despise God, to obey Him or to disobey Him. This commandment was true only because God commanded it—there was no human reasoning that could explain its existence. In other words, we can look at laws such as stealing and murder, and we can see that society runs smoother if such laws are kept; but there are many laws God has given through the ages that are to be obeyed, although human reasoning sees no explanation why.

God makes Eve (2:18-25):

Jehovah God said, "It is not good for the man to be alone. I will make him a companion suitable for his needs." God took the animals which He had formed and brought them to the man to let him call them what he would, and whatever man called them, that was their name. So the man named the cattle, the birds, and the beasts of the field—but among them all there was not a suitable companion found for Adam (man).

Jehovah God caused Adam to fall into a deep sleep, and He took a rib from his side and closed up the flesh, and from the bare bone and flesh of the rib, God made a woman and brought her to the man. When Adam saw her, he said, "This is now bone of my bone and flesh of my flesh. She will be called woman because she was taken from man." Later he named her Eve (3:20). For this reason *(that he needs a companion),* a man shall leave his father and mother and shall *cleave (adhere)* to his wife

Both the man and woman were naked, and were not ashamed.

God knew exactly what man needed. To perform the role God gave him and to enjoy life with all its manifold joys, he needed a female counterpart. This was no surprise to God. He brought all the animals before Adam so that Adam could realize how badly he needed a companion. In observing the animals, Adam could see that each male animal had its female counterpart, its partner.

When God brought the companion to Adam, he realized she was a part of himself because she was bone of his bone and flesh of his flesh. Therefore she was Ishshah" (Hebrew for woman) because she was taken from Ish" (Hebrew for man). Adam meant, "this is a female man," or, as we say in English, a woman.

This story is the foundation of the marriage relationship. The law set forth in Genesis 2:24 was not limited to the Garden of Eden, or to Adam and Eve, because Adam had no parents to leave. Jesus refers to the law of God "from the beginning" to correct the Jews' misconceptions about marriage and divorce (Matt. 19:4-5, 8). This verse states God's plan for marriage throughout time.

The First Sin
(Genesis 3:1-24)

The serpent was craftier than any beast of the field. One day when Eve was alone in the garden, the serpent said to her, "Is it actually true that God has forbidden you to eat of all the trees of the garden?"

Eve replied, "Of the fruit of the trees of the garden, we may eat, but of the fruit of the tree which is in the midst of the garden God has said, 'You shall not eat of it, or even touch it, lest you die.'"

The serpent said, "You will *not* surely die. God knows that when you eat of this fruit, your eyes will be opened, and you will be as God, knowing good and evil."

When Eve saw that the fruit of the tree looked as if it would taste good, that it was a beautiful fruit, and the serpent had said it was desirable to make her wise, she picked the fruit and ate it. She took some to her husband and he ate it also.

Then their eyes were opened, and they realized their nakedness. They sewed fig leaves together to make aprons to hide themselves. When they heard the sound of God walking in the garden in the late afternoon, they hid themselves among the trees from His presence.

In Hebrew, the question the serpent asked expresses surprise. Even at this, the beginning of Satan's activity with mankind, we find him living up to his name devil (accuser), because by his question he is accusing God of being completely unreasonable.

There can be no doubt that it was Satan who used the serpent as his tool to tempt and to beguile Eve. There is no reason to think that the serpent would have been any more likely to act the part of the devil than any other animal. If this temptation came from the serpent alone, then temptation and sin came into the world without Satan—but that does not fit the rest of the Bible. No, Satan chose to use the serpent because of his craftiness, but it was Satan at work (see John 8:44; Rom. 16:20; Rev. 12:9; 20:2).

Satan implied that God's motive in forbidding Adam and Eve to eat the fruit was to suppress them,

to keep them from being all they could be. This appeal has been the sirens' call to men ever since. God's ways are said to suppress men, to hold them back, to stifle them. In reality God' way sets men free while Satan's way brings men into abject slavery.

The temptation to Eve was along the same three avenues all temptations since have followed: the lust of the flesh (the fruit was desirable for food), the lust of the eyes (the fruit was a delight to the eyes), and the pride of life (the fruit was desirable to make one wise) (1 John 2:15-17).

The New Testament teaches that Eve was beguiled, not just tempted (1 Tim. 2:14; 2 Cor. 11:3). That is, she was deceived into thinking that the consequence of death would not follow the eating of the forbidden fruit. Adam was not deceived; he ate knowing that he was disobeying God, but he gave in to the temptation as human beings have in all generations since.

The fig leaves were literally leaves, not some other form of clothing. There had been no concept of clothing until this moment. Adam and Eve had not been wearing any covering—but neither had any other creature. So, in their innocence, the thought had never occurred. They did not feel naked. Now that guilt and shame and fear had come crushing in upon them, they felt their nakedness and attempted to cover themselves. Remember that the rest of us know well these feelings of guilt and shame by the time we become adults, but Adam and Eve were created adults and did not know these negative emotions at all. What a blow to have all these terrible feelings to come suddenly upon them!

Jehovah called to Adam and said, "Where are you?"

Adam answered, "I heard you in the garden, and I was afraid because I was naked, and hid myself."

"Who told you that you were naked?" God asked. "Have you eaten the fruit I told you not to eat?"

"The woman you gave me gave the fruit of the tree to me, and I ate it," Adam replied.

The Lord said to Eve, "What is this you have done?"

Eve replied, "The serpent deceived me, and I ate the fruit."

> **The first promise of a Savior (Gen. 3:15):**
>
> **"I will put enmity between you and the woman, between your seed and her seed. He will bruise your head and you will bruise His heel."**

Then God spoke to the serpent, "Because you have done this, you will be cursed above all the animals of the field. You will crawl upon your belly from this time forward and you will eat dust all the days of your life. And I will put enmity between you and the woman, between your seed and her seed. He will bruise your head and you will bruise His heel."

To the woman God said, "I will greatly multiply your pain in bearing children. Also, your desire will be subordinated to your husband, and he will rule over you."

Finally to Adam God said, "Because you have listened to your wife, and have eaten from the tree of which I told you not to eat, the ground will be cursed for your sake. By hard work you will produce the food you eat. The earth will bring forth thorns and thistles, and you will eat the vegetables of the field. By the sweat of your face you will eat your bread till you return to the ground, because from it you were taken, and to it you will return."

Adam called his wife Eve *(chavah—living or life)* because she was the mother of all human beings. And Jehovah God made coats of skins for Adam and Eve to wear.

Then God said, "Look, the man has become as one of us, to know good and evil. Now, let us take steps to keep him from eating from the Tree of Life and living forever." So God sent Adam forth from the garden to till the soil. At the entrance of the garden God put cherubim and the flame of a sword to keep man from going back to the Tree of Life.

The promise in Genesis 3:15 is very significant. The unfolding, the revealing, of the plan of redemption begins with this verse even though neither Adam, Eve, the serpent, nor Satan (see 1 Cor. 2:7-8) understood its full impact. It must not be overlooked in any study of the Bible.

Even though the surface reference is to the hatred between human beings and serpents, the deeper, more important significance is to the strife between the seed of woman, who is Christ, and Satan. At Christ's death He brought to nothing the power of Satan (bruised his head, a mortal wound—Heb. 2:14). Though Jesus was slain by the forces of evil, it was according to the plan and foreknowledge of God (Acts 2:23). Death itself proved to be temporary because He was raised from the dead (hence a bruised heel—a blow from which He recovered). On this early day when Eve sinned, Satan won the victory. The promise is that One would come, a descendant of woman, who would win the battle against Satan that Eve lost that day.

If words have any meaning at all, then serpents did not crawl before the fall of man. This form of travel was part of the curse. Since the passage also describes the serpent as being the most "subtil," (shrewdest) of all the creatures (3:1), then the removal of that subtlety must also have been part of the curse. This curse serves as a reminder of the entrance of sin, to help men remember that it was the serpent by which Satan beguiled Eve and brought sin into the world. Through that entrance of sin, paradise was lost on this earth.

The woman was subject to man to a degree before she sinned because man was made first and she was made for him. In 1 Corinthians 11:3, 8-9 where Paul discusses the subjection of the woman to man, he does not mention her transgression, but rather the order and purpose of her creation. Eve's transgression added another reason for her subjection: "Adam was not beguiled, but the woman being beguiled, has fallen into transgression" (1 Tim. 2:14). She did not use wisdom on this particular occasion, and therefore, her subjection was intensified as a result. Just as the crawling snake reminds us that Satan used the serpent in order to introduce sin into the world, so the role of submission for women to men is a reminder of Eve's role in the first sin. This subjection was a punishment to Eve, and a consequence of sin to all women who have lived since Eve.

Woman's subjection to man was stated here in the Garden of Eden after this first sin, and it was repeated in the New Testament, with specific reasons given for God's statements on the subject. The laws concerning woman's relationship and submission to man are still the same as they were in the New Testament, even in this day of rebellion against God's law on the subject. The same reasons exist, and God's laws have not been repealed. A married woman has a unique obligation to submit to her husband (Eph. 5:22-24; 1 Pet. 3:1-6), but all women must respect the command for a role of submission, of quietness, in their relationship to all men (1 Cor. 14:33b-35; 1 Tim. 2:11-12).

God appointed that a woman would have pain and discomfort in connection with child-bearing—not as a punishment to all women who came after Eve, but as a further reminder of the entrance of sin into the world.

Paradise with its ease, its comforts and its pleasures, including man's companionable association with God, were all lost. Now toil, old age, and death awaited Adam. Satan had told the truth in one point—they now knew evil as well as good—but what a sad knowledge it was!

Adam and Eve did not die physically the day they sinned, and it may look as if Satan told the truth on that point also. But look at death in a different way. Death is a separation—physical death is the separation of the spirit from the body. An even worse kind of death is spiritual death which is separation of man from God. So God was right. Spiritual death did occur the moment they ate of the tree. Never again would their relationship with God be the same.

God did not intend that man should live forever on this earth in the knowledge and practice of sin. Only when these sins were forgiven through the provisions God would make, and man would learn to put away the practice of sin, would he be given access to the Tree of Life again— this time in heaven itself (Rev. 2:7). From this point forward in history, mankind needed a Savior. They could not erase what they had done. They could not pay the price for sin themselves without dying and then having no more part in God's mercy. The rest of the Bible is the story of the coming of that Savior, and of God's plan to offer mankind a chance to be redeemed, to enjoy His blessings in spite of man's sin.

Cherubim are some kind of heavenly creatures who immediately wait upon God. They had wings (Exod. 25:20). For a description of cherubim, look at the visions Ezekiel had (Ezek. 1:4-28; 10:9-14). The description in Ezekiel, however, does not fit the description of the cherubim that were made to go on the top of the ark of the covenant (Exod 25:17-20), nor the ones made to go in the temple that Solomon built (1 Kings 6:23-28). There is no way to know, therefore, what these beings looked like at the entrance to the Garden of Eden. In fact, since the description of cherubim changes fairly drastically from passage to passage, the cherubim may not be actual, specific beings at all, but figures representing all creation as it serves Jehovah. It is not necessary for us to speculate about how the beings looked, but it is important for us to be impressed with the seriousness of sin. It was so serious Adam and Eve lost their right to live in the Garden of Eden and to eat from the Tree of Life. There can never be sin without serious consequences following.

Cain and Abel
(Genesis 4:1-24)

After a time Eve conceived, and a son was born. She named him Cain *(Qanah—to get)*, saying, "I have gotten a man with the help of Jehovah." Then she bore a son whom she called Abel *(vanity or worthlessness)*.

Abel became a shepherd while Cain became a farmer. As time passed, Cain brought an offering to the Lord from his crops. Abel brought a firstborn animal from his flocks. Jehovah accepted the offering of Abel, but He rejected Cain's sacrifice.

Cain became very angry, and Jehovah said to him, "Why are you so angry and sad? If you have good intentions you should be cheerful. But if not, then be careful because sin is waiting to pounce on you. Do not let it take you under its control."

Cain had a confrontation with Abel, and while they were in the field, Cain rose up and killed his brother. Later Jehovah asked Cain, "Where is your brother?"

Cain replied, "How should I know? Am I my brother's keeper *(as an animal keeper)?*"

"The voice of your brother's blood cries to me from the ground," God said. "Now you are cursed. The earth which opened its mouth to receive your brother's blood will not yield to you its full capacity when you till it. You will be a fugitive and a wanderer in the earth."

Cain answered, "My punishment is greater than I can bear. Look, you have driven me from this area, and I will be hidden from your face. Everyone who finds me will seek to kill me."

Jehovah said, "Anyone who kills Cain, vengeance will be taken upon him seven-fold." And the Lord appointed a sign for Cain so that those finding him would not kill him.

Cain went out from the presence of God and went into the land of banishment and wandering to the east of Eden where the family of Adam remained. After a time Cain had a son by his wife, and he named him Enoch. He built a city *(village)* and called it Enoch after his son.

Eve did not name her second son "worthless" because she thought him to be of no value. Rather, the word Abel took on that meaning because his death brought to nought any possibility of what he might have accomplished. It is much the same idea we express when we say, 'What a waste."

Speculations have been endless about why God accepted Abel's sacrifice and rejected Cain's. The Hebrew writer says that Abel offered his sacrifice by faith (Heb. 11:4), which means that he obeyed God in his sacrifice, completely in harmony with God's revelation. Cain did not. Since we do not have a record of precisely what that revelation had been from God, it is useless for us to speculate about exactly what was wrong with Cain's offering. We do know, however, that in all sacrifices specifically mentioned before the law of Moses, the substance offered was an animal (e.g., see Gen. 8:20; 15:9-11; 22:13).

The Bible does not give any hint what the sign upon Cain was. All of Cain's descendants died in the flood, so there is no way that sign could have been passed down through his descendants to the present day.

Who was Cain's wife? This burning question has been the subject of many hours of useless speculation. This is one of the many questions whose answer depends upon a very basic belief or unbelief of what the Bible says. The name of Cain's wife is not given, but her identity is established by necessary inference. Let us look at some of the verses that make her identity a necessary conclusion:

- *Once the process of creation was completed, there was no need for further special creations because God set in order the laws of procreation as He made each thing (1:11, 22, 28). Therefore, there was no need for God to create a special woman as a wife for Cain.*

- *A theory exists that says God created many people, not just Adam and Eve, and that Cain married one of those women. But that simply is **not** what the Bible teaches. Adam named his wife Eve because she was the mother of all living (3:20). Throughout the Bible, there are numerous passages that teach there was only one man and one woman created. Paul says that through "one man sin entered into the world" (Rom. 5:12). In an even more emphatic passage, Paul stated in his sermon on Mars Hill that 'He made from one, every nation of mankind to live on all the face of the earth..." (Acts 17:26). The theory cannot be true.*

- *Therefore, Cain married one of the only women in existence: his sister, or possibly even a niece, as Nahor married his niece Milcah (Gen. 11:27-29), and Abram married his half-sister (20:12). From the wording of the text, we all assume that Cain was the oldest son of Adam and Eve, but it is possible that the names of Cain and Abel are given because of the events that are told in the story. Adam lived to be 930 years old, and he had sons and daughters. People continued to marry their sisters or other very near relatives (see 24:3-4, 15; 28:1-2; 29:10), until many years later when the law of Moses was set in order by God (Lev. 18:6-18).*

The author of Genesis gives us the lineage of Cain's descendants for a time and then turns back to the narrative of the line of Adam's descendants which leads to the One who would come to fulfill the scheme of redemption.

Of Cain's descendants there was one Jabal who was the father *(the prototype, the first)* of those who dwell in tents and have cattle. Jubal was the forerunner of musicians. Tubal-cain was the first craftsman in metals.

Lamech married two wives and said to them, "Adah and Zillah, hear me: whoever tries to wound me or put a stripe on me, whether mature man or youth, I will put him to death. For every injury done to me, I will take ten times more vengeance than that with which God promised to avenge the murder of my ancestor Cain."

The evolutionists try to tell us that the first men (or half-men) were very ignorant and only learned basic skills over long periods of time. The Bible record is very different. Abel domesticated animals. Cain farmed. They each knew how to build a fire to offer their sacrifices. Cain's descendants lived in tents (man-made shelters), played musical instruments, and worked in metals. Adam could carry on a conversation with God from the very first, and he had the ability to care for the Garden of Eden because his first command was to dress and keep the garden. Obviously, therefore, God gave Adam a knowledge of a language of some kind and a knowledge of the first skills he needed for existence. Early man was as intelligent as modern men.

The story of Lamech illustrates another thing that began very early—men sought to forge their own destiny apart from God. They used the precious gift of intellect given them by God to accomplish their own goals and not God's. We see the spirit that has characterized man throughout his history: one of pride and arrogance, a spirit that says, "If you do anything to me, I will get revenge."

Generations of Adam
(Genesis 4:25-5:32)

After a time Eve had another son whom she called Seth because she said, "God has appointed me another son instead of Abel." To Seth a son was born named Enosh. Then men began to call on the name of Jehovah.

In other words, the descendants of Cain followed the ways of men while the descendants of Seth followed the ways of God. Thus the conflict between evil and righteous men intensified.

Memorize the generations from Adam to Noah:

Adam
Seth
Enos
Kenan (Cainan)
Mahalalel
Jared
Enoch
Methuselah
Lamech
Noah

Chapter 5 gives the generations of Adam, who was created at the beginning in the likeness of God.

We need to learn the generations as we go along because this is the lineage of Christ—this long before His coming! No human historian could have known which line to follow. Children learn such lists easily if the teacher will drill with them regularly.

The people had extraordinarily long life-spans during this earliest period of history. It seems reasonable that God planned it this way to allow rapid population growth, and perhaps to hasten the accumulation of experience and wisdom. The long lives may have been due to the healthier conditions of a new world and to the healthier bodies of people who were little removed from the perfect bodies of Adam and Eve. The only problem with this second explanation is that the life-spans dropped rapidly after the flood, so God must have had a direct hand in allowing them to live so long in this very early period rather than its just being some natural phenomenon. This is the only period of history when men lived nearly a thousand years. We do know that these years were actual years, as we understand them, not half-years or months or some other short cycles. Even the earliest men could tell the cycle of the seasons and counted their years accordingly.

Enoch is the character who stands out in this list of generations because he is one of only two men who never died. The other man was Elijah (2 Kings 2). The Hebrew writer uses Enoch as an example of faith (Heb. 11:5-6). Enoch walked with God; he pleased God, but one cannot please God without faith, therefore the Hebrew writer says that he walked by faith and was taken to heaven without dying.

Methuselah is listed as living the longest of all—969 years. Next to him was Jared, 962 years. There may have been others alive at that same time who are not listed in this genealogy who lived as long or longer. If we take the time Methuselah lived after he begat Lamech, we have the figure of 782 years (5:26). If we take Lamech's age when he begat Noah (182 years), and add that to the age of Noah when the flood came (600 years), we come out with the matching figure of 782 years, indicating that Methuselah died the year of flood. *We must be very cautious, however, in trying to establish an exact time frame from lists of generations. There are numerous times in the Bible when generations were skipped in a genealogy list. These lists are given to show which family a particular individual fits into, not to show an exact record of the passing of time. For more study on this point, compare the list of the generations of Jesus in Matthew 1:1-17 to the list of the kings of Judah from the books of Kings and Chronicles. Some of the kings are skipped, but every one of the rulers of the kingdom of Judah were direct ancestors of the Christ except Athaliah, Jehoahaz, and Zedekiah. (See Lesson 8, pages 29-34 of The History and Geography of the Bible Story, by Bob and Sandra Waldron, for a further discussion of dating Bible events.)*

Noah's Sons:

Shem
Ham
Japheth

Noah was five hundred years old when he is introduced in the story. He was the father of three sons: Shem, Ham, and Japheth.

The Flood
(Genesis 6:1-9:29)

Mankind becomes wicked (6:1-4):

As men multiplied upon the face of the earth, and daughters were born unto them, the sons of God noted their beauty and married their particular choices among them.

And Jehovah said, "My Spirit will not rule in man for ever; in their wandering they show they are of the flesh. Therefore his days shall be 120 years."

There were tyrants in the earth in those days, and also afterward, when the sons of God went in unto the daughters of men and had children by them. These were the famous heroes of legend.

Let us reject the unfounded interpretations that some men have placed on these verses, namely that the sons of God were angels, that they married women and produced a race of giants. While it is true that angels are on occasion referred to as sons of God (Job 1:6), never are they shown as beings who could mate with human women. There is nothing in this passage or anywhere else in the Scriptures to indicate this theory is true.

The primary point being established in this passage is how wicked the world had become. It was not with angels that God became so angry He decided to destroy them. It was men.

The expression "took wives" is used in the Bible of the marriage relationship, not merely physical connection. There is no evidence that angels by their own power could take upon themselves flesh and live as human beings. Jesus Himself pointed out that angels neither marry nor are given in marriage (Matt. 22:30).

The passage is saying that there came to be intermarriage between the wicked and the righteous—possibly between the descendants of Cain and the descendants of Seth. At first they were separate because Cain had been driven away, but as the people multiplied, they were thrown together again, and when that happened, intermarriage between the spiritually-minded and the worldly-minded—between the righteous and the wicked, began to occur and, as a result, wickedness spread.

Numerous times in Bible history marriage to the wrong people proved to be disastrous. In the law of Moses, God forbade the Israelites to marry the Canaanites (Deut. 7:3-4). The writer here is making the point that the sons of God—those among whom the worship of the true God had been kept alive—began their apostasy by choosing wives without regard to their moral and spiritual inclinations. Instead of marrying the "daughters of God," they married the "daughters of men." Spiritual concerns were cast aside; only the beauty of the women was considered.

Of course, Adam and Eve had other sons and daughters (Gen. 5:4), and it is unlikely that all of them were righteous people. As the years passed, likely wickedness cropped up among Seth's descendants also. Regardless of exactly who they were, it is best to assume that the sons of God were those who until this point had walked in God's ways, and the daughters of men were those who had long since abandoned God's ways.

God determined that He would not endlessly go on seeking to guide men by His Spirit here before the flood. A limit was placed upon such efforts—the remaining days would be 120 years. The length of time does not refer to the lifetime men would experience because there was no point in history when 120 years became the standard length of life for men. The 120 years was the length of time left before the flood, and since the flood began in the six hundredth year

of Noah (7:6), this determination of God was made when Noah was 480 years old This 120 years was when the longsuffering of God waited in the days of Noah, "while the ark was a preparing" (1 Pet. 3:20). It was also the time when Noah, "preacher of righteousness," did his preaching and warning (2 Pet. 2:5).

The word Nephilim in verse 4 comes from the word Naphal and means lo fall, to fall upon as an oppressor. "It does not necessarily mean giant in the sense that we understand the word. Giants could be Nephilim (tyrants, oppressors; see Num. 13:33), but Nephilim could be tyrants without being giants. Nothing in the present context points to enormous size.

God warns Noah to prepare for the flood (6:5-22):

Jehovah saw that mankind had become exceedingly wicked; his every thought was evil; and God regretted that He had made man upon the earth. God grieved over the matter, and He said, "I will blot out man whom I have created from the face of the earth; I will also destroy every animal, every creeping thing, and every bird of the sky."

But in the midst of all the wickedness, there was Noah who found favor in the eyes of the Lord. So God said to Noah:

I have seen the wickedness which fills the earth, and the end of all flesh has come before me. I am planning to destroy them from the earth. Make an ark (literally a "box," a barge) of gopher wood. Build rooms in the ark and pitch it within and without with tar. The length shall be 450 feet, the width 75 feet, and the height 45 feet. Prepare an opening in the side of the ark for light one cubit from the roof. Divide the interior into lower, second, and third stories.

I intend to bring a flood of water upon the earth to destroy every living thing that breathes. But I will make my covenant (my contract) with you, and you will get into this ark, you and your wife, your sons and their wives. Take with you two of every kind of animal, the male and its female, into the ark. Of the birds, and of the cattle, and of every crawling thing, two of every kind will come to you, for you to keep them alive. Take food of every kind and store it for you and for the animals.

Noah did exactly as God had commanded him.

The shape of the ark is obvious from the meaning of the word "ark" a box or chest; but beyond that, the details of design are unclear. The ark was very large, containing 101,250 square feet of floor space on the three decks. The total volume was 1,518,750 cubic feet. The interior was divided into an unspecified number of rooms or compartments.

The number of animals Noah had on the ark is not given, but the task of gathering them and caring for them was a big one. But Noah did not need to gather, for example, all kinds of dogs—but rather one pair. The total number of animals would have been reduced considerably by this measure. It may be that they took the young of the larger animals. Notice that God said the animals and birds would come to Noah (6:20), so He did not leave it for Noah to hunt and choose which animals to save. We need not concern ourselves with how they accomplished what God had commanded. Noah obeyed God and saved the animal life God wanted saved, and God used His power to help preserve life on board the ark, while at the same time using His power to destroy life outside the ark.

Beware of any theory that tells "exactly" how the flood occurred—whether an icy meteor coming into the earth's atmosphere, or something else. The Bible does not tell us. God may have used some phenomenon of nature to bring about the flood at the exact moment He wanted it to arrive, or He may have devised some specific, one-time measure by which there could be this much rain within these forty days, but there is no way to determine exactly how He chose to do it. Faith demands that we believe the Bible record as it stands and refuse to speculate about details not given.

The flood begins (7:1-24):

Finally the time came for the flood to begin so God said to Noah, "It is time for you and for all your family to come into the ark, for I have found you righteous before me in this generation. Of every clean animal, take seven males and seven females, and of the unclean animals, two of each kind, the male and his female, in order to keep seed alive upon the earth. Take the birds of the sky by sevens also. Seven days from now I will cause it to

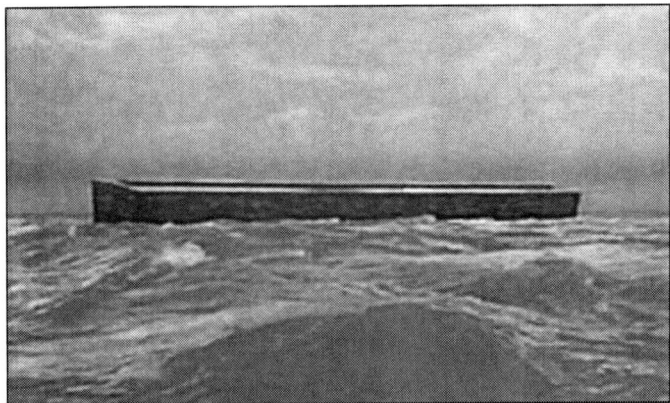

rain upon the earth, and the rain will continue for forty days and forty nights, and I will destroy every living thing from the earth." So Noah did exactly as God commanded.

This is the first time that "clean" and "unclean" animals are mentioned. No details are given here to distinguish between them—although it is obvious Noah had information that is not recorded, in order to know which fit into which category. As the history proceeds, it will become obvious that the "clean" animals were the ones they offered as sacrifices to God This is why more clean animals were needed to sustain their kind after the flood.

Noah was six hundred years old when the flood came upon the earth. It began on the seventeenth day of the second month of Noah's six hundredth year. The fountains of the great oceans were loosed, and the windows of heaven were opened, and the rain fell for forty days and forty nights just as God predicted.

The mountains of Ararat.

The waters rose above the earth, and the ark was borne upon the surface of the waters. The water continued to rise until the tops of even the highest mountains were covered. All the high mountains that were under the whole heaven were covered. The water even rose fifteen cubits above the mountains, and all life which breathes upon the earth perished, both men, and cattle, and birds—everything. Only Noah was left, and those with him in the ark. The water held its level for 150 days.

We can imagine the scorn, the scoffing, and the unbelief of Noah's generation. How surprised they must have been when the rain started—and think how quickly their scorn turned to horror as the heavy rains began and continued day after day. The ark had stood upon its supports, huge, silent, and wet with rain until the day it lifted from those supports and began to float. Meanwhile, in a storm such as the world has known only this once, the waters overflowed first from the rivers and lakes, and then from the oceans themselves. As the waters rose, men and women, along with the animals, sought for higher ground— until there was none left. After only a few weeks, think what a scene of desolation the earth must have presented! In our mind's eye, we can see the ark floating alone upon the water's surface, almost obscured by the falling sheets of rain. Even when the rain stopped, the waters remained high 110 more days.

Notice the wording of the text: "...and all the high mountains that were under the whole heaven were covered" (7: 19). This strongly indicates it was a world-wide flood. Arguments have been made that mankind had not yet spread all over the earth, and therefore, the flood was only in the small area where people were living. The problem is that this theory does not fit with the wording of the passages. The "fountains of the great deep" (the oceans) were opened (7:11); the highest mountains under the whole heaven were covered (7:19); every living thing that was upon the face of the earth died, except for those within the ark (7:21-23). If there had been animal life left upon the earth in places beyond the range of the flood, then Noah would not have needed to take animals into the ark in order to preserve life.

Some argue that it had never rained before the flood because this is the first time rain is mentioned by that term—but this theory is not reasonable. God set in motion all the laws of nature when He made and organized the earth and the heavens. Back in 2:5-6, one of the reasons given for the lack of growth of the plants at that point was that it had not yet rained. Then the very next verse tells that a mist arose from the earth and watered the whole face of the ground. That is an exact, though simple, description of the laws controlling the process of evaporation, the formation of clouds, and rain. The same word translated "mist" is used in Job 36:27 of the cycle of evaporation and rain.

The flood waters recede (8:1-22):

God did not forget Noah, his family, and all the animal life with them. He caused a wind to pass over the earth, and the waters gradually went down. On the seventeenth day of the seventh month (*five months after the rains began*), the ark rested on Mount Ararat. The water continued to decrease, and on the first day of the tenth month the tops of the mountains could be seen.

After forty more days, Noah opened the window of the ark and set a raven free. The raven *(a stronger bird)* flew here and there until the waters were dried up from the earth. Then Noah sent out a dove, but the dove found no place to light and soon returned to the ark. Noah reached out and brought it back into the ark. Seven days later he sent the dove out again. This time she came back with a freshly picked olive leaf in her beak, so Noah knew that the waters were nearly gone and that plant life had begun to grow again. Another week passed, and Noah sent the dove out once more, and this time she did not return.

Do you see that Noah could not look out of the ark and see the condition of the ground for himself? He had to send birds out for these first examinations. Do you also see that God did not bring about a new creation of plant life or animal life? It was rebuilt by the natural laws of nature that God had ordained.

On the first day of the first month of Noah's six hundred and first year, the waters were dried up from the earth. Noah removed the covering of the ark, and he could see that the earth's surface was dry *(that is, there was no standing water).* It was in the second month, on the twenty-seventh day of the month, that the earth was completely dry. *(How long had it been since they entered the ark?)*

God spoke to Noah and said, "Come out of the ark, you and your family. Bring out the animals you put on the ark so that they can breed abundantly upon the earth."

Noah built an altar unto the Lord and took one of every clean beast and of every clean bird and offered burnt offerings upon the altar. God was pleased and said to Himself, "I will not again curse the ground for man's sake because of his wickedness. Neither will I destroy everything living as I have just done.

"As long as the earth remains,
seedtime and harvest,
cold and heat,
summer and winter,
day and night
shall not cease."

God's covenant with Noah (9:1-17):

With Noah and his family, God was starting over with humanity. He blessed them and said, "Be fruitful and multiply and fill the earth," just as He had commanded Adam and Eve in the beginning (1:28). The dominion that man had been given over the creation is expressed even more strongly to Noah than to Adam: "The fear of you and the dread of you will be upon every wild animal and upon every bird. Every moving thing that lives will be for food. As I have before given you the vegetation to eat, so I now give you meat. Only you are not to eat the blood of the animal. I will require a penalty when your blood is shed by an animal or by a man. Whoever kills a man, will in turn be killed, because God made man in His own image.

"Whoever sheds man's blood,
by man his blood shall be shed,
For in the image of God He made man."

God continued speaking to Noah, saying, "Look, I am establishing my covenant with you and with your descendants after you, as well as with all living creatures. I will never again destroy every living thing through a flood. As a sign of this covenant, I am setting my rainbow in the cloud to serve as a reminder of the pact between me and the earth. From now on, when I bring a cloud upon the earth, the rainbow will be visible in the cloud. Then you will know that I am remembering my agreement between me and you and every living creature. No more will the waters become a flood to destroy every living thing."

Many environmentalists and animal rights activists do not view man as master of the creation, the one to whom the creation was subjected, and for whom it was made. They view man as merely one of the animals who has become a terrible villain, a vicious monster to the other creatures. Though man has done much to pollute and misuse the creation, and though his cruelty to animals, as well as to other men, has often been unbounded, yet the basic position of the environmentalists and animal rights activists is out of harmony with what the Bible says about man's position in the creation.

Notice that meat is added to the diet at this time. Immediately after the creation, plants were given to men and animals as their food (1:29-30). This is the first time meat is added as food All animals, "every moving thing that is alive," were included (9:3). No rules were given about clean or unclean animals, such as were given in the law of Moses (see Lev. 11). Those rules restricting which animals could be eaten were repealed in the New Testament when God showed Peter in vision that he must not consider things unclean which God had cleansed (Acts 10:10-15). In Acts 15, the only restriction placed upon the food proper for Gentile Christians to eat was to "abstain from things strangled and from blood" (Acts 15:20, 29). "Things strangled" refers to animals killed in a way that did not bleed them thoroughly.

There are two more important points to be noted here. One is the prohibition against eating blood This prohibition is included in every age of God's dealing with mankind It is specifically prohibited here in the patriarchal age as animals were added to man's diet for the first time (Gen. 9:4). The rule is repeated in the law of Moses (Lev. 17:10-14; Deut. 12:16, 23-25), and in the law of Christ (Acts 15:29). Occasionally someone says that we have now been loosed from this prohibition. But who loosed us? When was it done? This prohibition is rooted in the most profound concepts of Scripture. Blood was associated with the life of the creature (Gen. 9:4; Lev. 17:11; Deut. 12:23). Life is the most precious possession one has to give; it is the price God required for man's redemption. This prohibition was a way of enhancing and preserving the value of life in man's estimation. It is God's plan for that value, that estimation, to be observed throughout time.

The second point is closely related to the prohibition against eating blood Murder is prohibited here by God, and the penalty for murder is death. The reason for this penalty is not deterrence; it is justice. The sin of murder must have a penalty consistent with the crime. The only penalty sufficient is the death of the murderer. In this way the sanctity and value of human life is upheld. God is the giver of life, the creator of man. Only He has the right to take life. He is the One who commands that the murderer be executed

Notice however, that God did not inflict capital punishment upon Cain when he murdered his brother Abel. Some say that God's moral laws have never changed, but that simply is not true. God Himself was the One who punished Cain by banishing him from his family; now it is God Himself who is setting capital punishment, death, as the penalty for murder. God's laws fit into a particular dispensation only if He includes that law in that particular covenant with man. Here in Genesis 9 it is given in the patriarchal age; it is repeated in the law of Moses (Exod. 21:12-14; Lev. 24:17; Num. 35:3 1-33; Deut. 19:13); and again in the law of Christ (Acts 25:11; Rom. 1:32; 13:1-4), but it did not begin until after the flood

A curse is placed upon Canaan (9:18-29):

Now the sons of Noah were Shem, Ham, and Japheth. From these came the population of the whole earth. The first of these descendants to be mentioned is Ham's son Canaan.

When life resumed its normal course after the flood, Noah became a farmer, and he planted a vineyard. When he drank the wine of his grapes, he became drunk and was lying in his tent unclothed. Ham saw his father's nakedness and told his two brothers outside. Shem and Japheth put a garment *(robe or cloak)* upon their shoulders and went into the tent backward, so as not to see their father's nakedness, and laid the garment upon Noah.

When Noah recovered from his drunkenness and learned what his younger son had done, he placed a curse upon Canaan, the son of Ham, saying:

> "Cursed be Canaan;
> A servant of servants
> will he be to his brethren.
> Blessed be the Lord, the God of Shem;
> and let Canaan be his servant.
> May God enlarge Japheth,
> and let him dwell in the tents of Shem,
> and let Canaan be his servant."

Noah lived after the flood 350 years to the age of 950, and he died. Noah is the last man in the Bible who is recorded as living more than 900 years. The life-span of men rapidly decreased after the flood.

The Hebrew of verse 20 is best rendered: "And Noah the husbandman (or farmer) began and planted a vineyard." Therefore, some scholars assume that Noah was the first to cultivate the grape and did not know the danger of intoxication. This supposition might be true, but it is a little hard to believe that in all the years before the flood no one had eaten grapes and discovered how delicious they are. If men before the flood had ever done so, then the likelihood is that their cultivation of the vine followed, and with it, the inevitable discovery of grape juice and wine.

All verse 20 is saying is that after the flood, Noah, as a farmer, began cultivating the vine. Noah would not have gotten drunk unless he had drunk a large quantity of fermented grape juice. He was, therefore, guilty of intemperance which led to drunkenness. The Bible tells the truth about even the heroes of faith—including their times of imperfections as well as their times of strength. The emphasis in this passage is upon the sin of Ham, which was a lack of respect for his father, and the prophetic curse against Ham's descendants through his son Canaan that followed.

The curse made here will come true in a very literal way as we follow the history in the next few

books of the Bible. Canaan's descendants made their home in the little fertile strip of land on the south-eastern edge of the Mediterranean Sea. This was the very land God subsequently promised to the descendants of Abraham, who were the descendants of Shem. And indeed, Abraham's descendants, the Israelites, took the land of Canaan with God's help and made the remaining Canaanites their slaves.

Eventually, the Gentiles, the descendants of Japheth, came to share the tents of Shem. It is best to understand this blessing conferred upon Japheth as a sharing of the spiritual blessings of Shem in Christ in whom both Jew and Gentile are made one (Eph. 2:19-16). Shem and Japheth both behaved honorably in the treatment of their father and are both blessed in contrast to the curse placed upon Ham (and specifically upon his son Canaan). Therefore, the statement regarding Japheth should not be taken as implying a curse upon Shem (such as the forcible taking of the dwellings of Shem), but as a sharing of his blessings.

The Scattering of the People
(Genesis 10:1-11:32)

The generations of the sons of Noah (10:1-32):

Before continuing with the narrative of history, the writer takes time to tell briefly where the descendants of each branch of Noah's family settled Chapter 10 gives an overview of the origins of different people that we will meet as we move forward in history. Look at the table that is given at the end of this section to see the nations that can be identified from each of these sons. Look at the map to see a general picture of where the descendants of each son settled.

No human historian could have known which of these sons of Noah to follow in the narrative, but the Bible record was not left to man's devising. Chapter 10 summarizes what happened to each of the sons of Noah and their descendants. Chapter 11 continues the narrative for one event that affected the whole human race, and then the record will narrow the lineage much more sharply. We will be brought back to the descendants of Shem—and specifically to the line through Eber's son Peleg, until we come to a man named Abram—to continue the divine history of the preparation for the coming of a Savior into the world. The historical note is given that it was in the days of Peleg, the son of Eber, that the events at the Tower of Babel occurred (10:25). These families of Shem, Ham, and Japheth, therefore, were all still together for several generations before they were divided at the Tower of Babel.

The descendants of Japheth (10:1-5):

The sons of Japheth were Gomer, Magog, Madai, Javan, Tubal, Meshach, and Tiras. There is much uncertainty about who the descendants of the sons of Japheth were. Gomer may have been the ancestor of the Cimmerians mentioned by Herodotus the historian. Magog is mentioned by Ezekiel in connection with Meshech and Tubal (Ezek. 38:1-3; 39:1). These were nomadic peoples who lived in northern Armenia and lands to the south and east of there. Those called Scythians would fit into this group. Madai is the ancestor of the Medes who become important to the Bible story very late in Old Testament history (see Isa. 13:17; Dan. 5:28, 30-31). Javan is the ancestor of the Ionians from whom the Greeks came.

Of the three sons of Gomer, Togarmah is the only one whose descendants can be identified with any certainty. They are the Armenians who are still called the Thorgom or Torkomatsi.

Of the sons of Javan, we can be fairly certain that Tarshish has to do with the colony of Tartessus in southern Spain. According to history, this colony is of Phoenician origin *(the Phoenicians descended from Ham, rather than Japheth)*, but this fact does not mean there were no native people in Tarshish when the Phoenicians established a trading post there. Kittim refers to people of the islands of the Mediterranean, particularly those on the island later known as Cyprus.

One reason it is very difficult to know who the descendants of Japheth were from this early list is that his descendants are the ones farthest removed from the Bible story itself Therefore, we know almost nothing about the early history of these people. Japheth's descendants mostly moved to the north and then to the east and west after the events connected with the Tower of Babel.

The descendants of Ham (10:6-20):

The sons of Ham were: Cush, Mizraim, Put, and Canaan. The descendants of Put are not specified.

Cush is the general name for the Ethiopians who lived south of the land of Egypt. Some of his descendants were found in Arabia also. Nimrod was a prominent early descendant of Cush. He became a man of great power in the earth; he was a mighty hunter and he became a builder of cities and kingdoms. He built Babel, Erech, Accad, and Calneh—all cities in the land of Shinar. From Shinar he moved north-westward into Assyria and founded the cities of Nineveh, Rehoboth-Ir, Caleh, and Resen.

Mizraim is the name for Egypt in the Hebrew language. It is likely that the name of this son was not originally in this form, because Mizraim is a noun of the dual form in Hebrew, and refers to Egypt as the land of *two* nations: upper and lower Egypt. The name of this son was probably something like Mizre. The descendants of Mizraim were primarily tribes of various parts of Egypt. The Philistines are listed as descendants of the Casluhim. The explanation given by Keil and Delitzsch is very sensible *(Keil & Delitzsch, vol. 1, pg. 129-130)*. The early Philistines (Gen. 26:1) were a colony of the Egyptian Casluhim. Later, during the period of the judges, this colony was greatly strengthened by a massive invasion of sea peoples from Caphtor (the Island of Crete) (see Jer. 47:4).

The descendants of Canaan include: Sidon, after whom the Phoenician city was named; Heth, from whom the Hittites came; and the various tribes which inhabited greater Palestine. It is interesting that though the Canaanites were Hamitic *(from Ham)* by race, their language, which became the language known as Hebrew, was of Semitic *(from Shem)* origin, as were most of the languages of Mesopotamia, Arabia, and Canaan. The term Canaanites included both the people of Canaan proper and the Phoenicians (10:19).

Though some of Ham's descendants moved into the lower regions of Arabia, and some into what was known as Asia Minor in New Testament days (specifically the Hittites), most of them moved into the continent of Africa. The Bible story tells about various descendants of Ham—but only as they come in contact with the Israelites who were descendants of Shem.

The descendants of Shem (10:21-32):

Shem's sons were Elam, Asshur, Arphaxad (*Arphachshad,—ASV*), Lud, and Aram. Elam's descendants settled just northeast of the Persian Gulf, and Biblical history refers to the land of Elam on different occasions. From Aram came a group of oft-mentioned people of the Old Testament, the Aramaeans *(their name is translated as Syrians in the King James Version)*. These were not all one nation of people, but rather a collection of tribes that had a close relationship in blood-lines and in their political holdings. Shem is referred to as the ancestor of all the children of Eber (through Arphaxad) because Eber was the father of two sons from whom descended, on the one hand Abraham and all his descendants, and on the other hand all the Arabian families of Joktan.

Chapter 11 will bring us back to the descendants of Shem in order to follow the particular line through his son Arphaxad to bring us to the family of Terah and his son Abram.

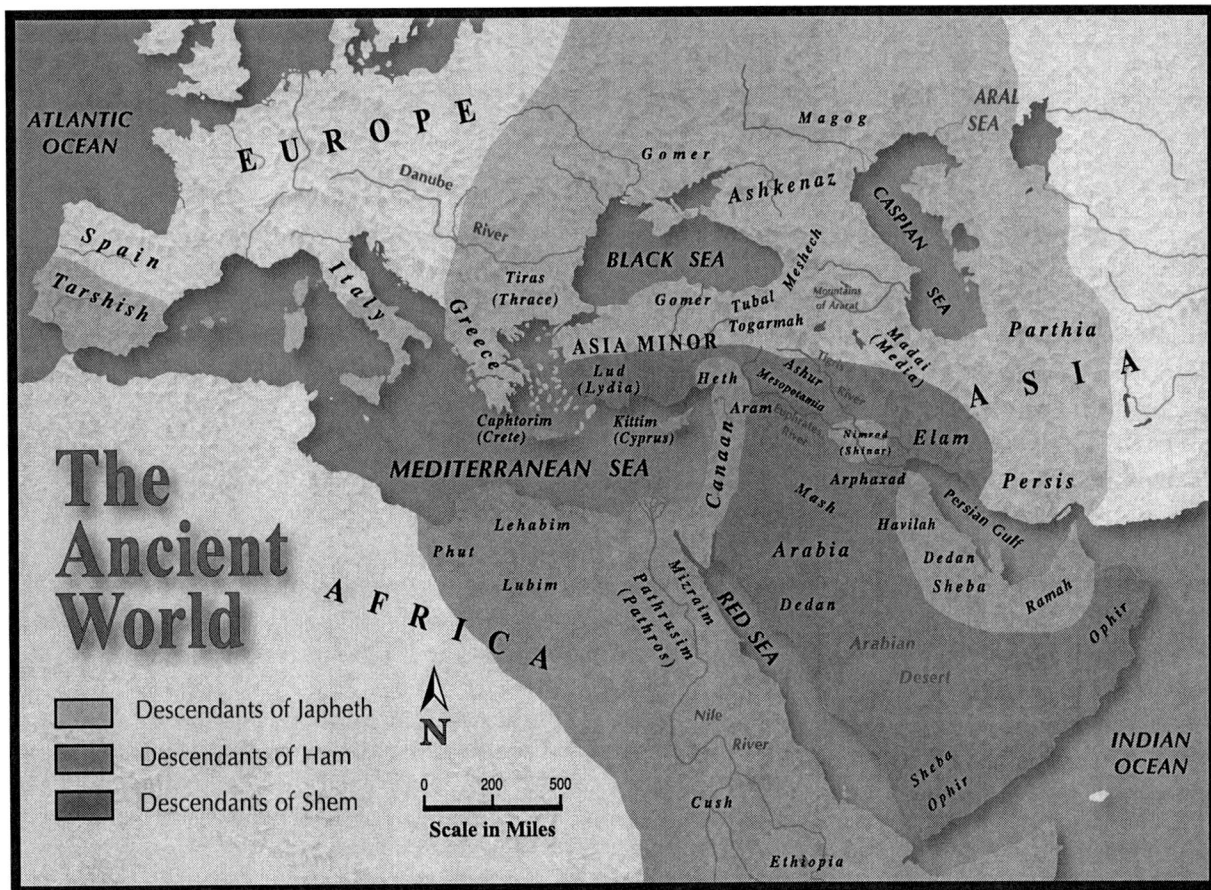

MAP ONE

Descendants of Shem	Descendants of Ham	Descendants of Japheth
Assyrians	Ethiopians	Javen:
Elamites	Egyptians	Greeks
Chaldeans	Lybians	Italians
Kingdom of Lydia	Canaanites:	Spanish
Aramaeans (Syrian tribes)	Sidonians	Isle of Cyprus (Kittim)
Arabian tribes	Hittites (Heth)	Medes (Madai)
Israelites	Jebusites	Persians
Edomites	Amorites	Parthians
Moabites	Girgashites	
Ammonites	Hivites	
	Southern Arabians	
	Early Babylonians	
	Philistines	

The Tower of Babel (11:1-9)

Chapter 10 tells *where* these earliest people settled, and the story of the Tower of Babel of chapter 11 tells *why* they scattered. The descendants of Noah came down from the high mountains of Ararat, traveling through the broad valley of Mesopotamia between the two rivers, the Tigris and the Euphrates. They were of one language and one family. As they moved southeastward they came to the land of Shinar, and on that plain they began to build a tower of baked brick and asphalt.

Notice that the bricks used in building the Tower of Babel were baked (burned). Baked bricks were much more durable than sun-dried ones. These bricks were put together with slime or tar, a petroleum based substance which was used as mortar and as water-proofing (see Exod. 2:3). The word is most commonly translated "slime. "Pitch, which was

Map Assignment:

Find the mountains of Ararat on your map. Notice that Ararat is a range of mountains. No one knows exactly which peak was the resting place of the ark. From there find the Tigris and Euphrates rivers and follow them southward to see that they almost come together where the city of Babylon was later built. Then they spread apart again until they come together to flow into the Persian Gulf. Shinar was just south of Babylon, in the upper part of that region where the rivers spread apart. Amraphel was king of Shinar in Abraham's day, many years after this story (Gen. 14:1).

sometimes used for water-proofing, was a substance like pine resin.

Though the shape of the Tower of Babel is not described, there are remains of a number of very early towers in the area of Mesopotamia. It is interesting to think it may have looked like one of these ancient ziggurats. Most such towers were built as temple towers, built solid with a temple on top. They were shaped like a pyramid in successive levels, with staircases ascending the outside. The remains of more than two dozen such towers are known today. The tower of Ur, as one example, stood about seventy feet high. The inside was made of sunbaked brick; the outside consisted of about eight feet of baked brick set in bitumen (slime). There is a record left of the building of this tower, called the Stele of Ur-Nammu (the name of the king). He ruled from 2112 to 2095 BC Therefor.e the ziggurat which is in ruins at Ur today (modern Iraq) would have been almost new when Abraham lived there, but remember that Abraham lived many years after the tower of Babel was started and then left unfinished No one can prove that any of the existing ruins date back to this tower—rather, the possibility of its lasting until the present are very remote. This event was still very, very early in the history of the world. (Information from Zondervan Pictorial Bible Dictionary, 913, and The Ancient Near East by James B. Pritchard, 31.)

The people encouraged one another saying, "Let us build a city and a tower whose top will reach into the heavens, and let us make a memorial here lest we be scattered over all the earth."

Jehovah came down to see the city and the tower which was being built *(that is, He observed what the people did)*. Having seen it, He said, "Look, they are one people, and speak one language. This is only the beginning of what they will do. When they have finished this, nothing they decide to do will be impossible for them. Come, let us go down and confound their language so that they will not understand one another's speech."

Therefore God caused the people to be unable to understand one another's speech, and they stopped building the city and scattered in different directions. So the city was called Babel, that is, "Confusion."

The restored ziggurat of Ur-Nammu in modern Iraq.

The people were determined to be united, and to this end they planned to build this great tower. The expression "make us a name" is used throughout the Old Testament to mean "to establish a reputation, to make a memorial."

It was God's will that men scatter over the earth (9:1), but there seems to be more involved in the command than God's merely wanting the earth populated Notice in verse 6 that God said if the people stayed together nothing would be restrained from them that they might imagine doing. His opposition was not to unity itself, but to what He saw they might do with their unity. It was not a threat to God personally, whatever man may have done, but it was a threat to His plan for mankind. Perhaps the wickedness of the people would have grown beyond measure had they all remained one, whereas, with the nations separated, some would not be as abased as others. From this moment forward in history, there has never been one global empire. This story is not only the beginning of different languages, but also the beginning of nationalism and of the differ-

ent cultures of man. Nationalism has proven to be a most potent element in keeping men from being one.

No one knows what the original language of man was. Neither is it known what families of language began here at the Tower of Babel. Certainly our modern languages were not created then. They are of much more recent origin.

The generations of Shem—Narrowed to one line (11:10-26):

Now the inspired historian comes back to the lineage of Shem and takes the particular line through which the scheme of redemption will unfold Remember that all such genealogy lists are given in order to show which family a particular individual came through, rather than being given to show the exact time an event happened

Practice this list of ten names together in your class, adding it to the list of ten generations given from Adam through Noah. This is a continuation of the lineage of the Christ. No particular points need to be emphasized except where some additional fact about the person is given in the Bible text. Notice how quickly the length of life shortens in this list. Noah was the last to live more than 900 years; Shem lived 602 years; Arphaxad lived 438 years; and Terah lived 205 years. By the days of David in the Old Testament, he died as an "old" man at about 70 years of age.

Three characters from this list need to be mentioned: Eber, Peleg, and Terah.

Eber is mentioned in 10:21, and we noted there that he was the ancestor of both the Israelites and the Arabian tribes. Chapter 11:10-15 makes it plain that there were some generations between

Memorize the generations from Shem to Abraham:

Shem
Arphaxad
Shelah (Salah)
Eber
Peleg
Reu
Serug
Nahor
Terah
Abraham

Shem and Eber, but he is mentioned in chapter 10 because he is the one of Shem's descendants whose family would play such an important part in the history soon to be told.

It was in the days of Peleg *(division)* that the story of the Tower of Babel occurred. If all the generations are named, then the evidence from this passage indicates that the events surrounding the Tower of Babel occurred about 100 years after the flood. Calculations have been done that if there were only 100 years between the flood and the tower, then there were probably about 30,000 people in existence at that time *(K & D., vol. 1, p. 136)*. That would probably fit the circumstances since it was before the people began scattering. Remember, however, that all such figuring about these earliest events is guesswork at best. God included only the information from this earliest period that was of universal importance. Even though many years passed between creation and the call of Abraham, almost nothing is revealed about the history of the period—only the creation itself, the first sin, Cain and Abel, the flood, and the scattering of the people. Other people are named to help us know how the different families and races came about, and ultimately into which family the Messiah fit.

Terah is introduced as the son of Nahor and the father of Abram, Nahor, and Haran. Genesis 20:12 tells that he was also the father of Sarai. Now that this particular family is introduced, the historian moves immediately into the history of one of Terah's sons, Abram.

The Patriarchs
(Genesis 11:27-50:26)

Abraham
(Genesis 11:27-25:18)

Generations of Terah (11:27-32):

As Moses moves from one division of his inspired history to another, he often uses the expression: "Now these are the generations of ..." (see 5:1; 6:9; 10:1; 11:10; 11:27; 25:19; 37:2). As we come to 11:27-32, Moses is ready to narrow the line of Noah, through Shem, even further to bring us to the lineage of one man: Abraham. So, though he labels this little section, "Now these are the generations of Terah...," almost immediately he singles out one of Terah's sons, Abram, in order to follow the story of his life. Therefore we are placing this short section here in our outline as a prologue to the story of Abraham.

Terah begat Abram, Nahor, and Haran. Haran begat Lot, Milcah, and Iscah and then died while the family still lived in Ur of the Chaldees. Abram and Nahor took wives for themselves: Abram married his half-sister Sarai (see 20:12), and Nahor married his niece Milcah. From the first, Sarai was barren, so she had no child.

Terah arose and took Abram, Lot, and Sarai from Ur to go into the land of Canaan. When they reached Haran in Paddan-aram they dwelt there. Terah lived a total of 205 years and died in Haran.

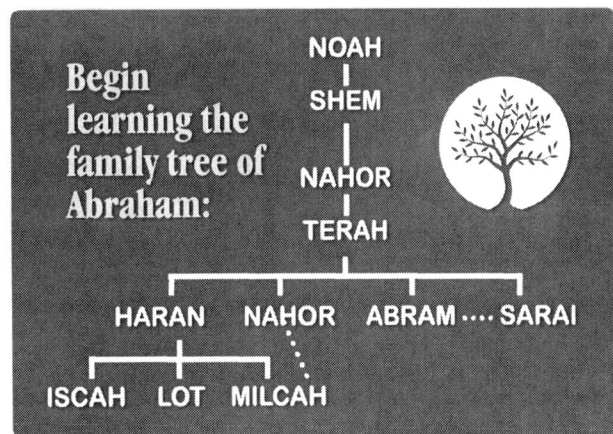

Begin learning the family tree of Abraham:

NOAH
SHEM
NAHOR
TERAH

HARAN   NAHOR   ABRAM ···· SARAI

ISCAH   LOT   MILCAH

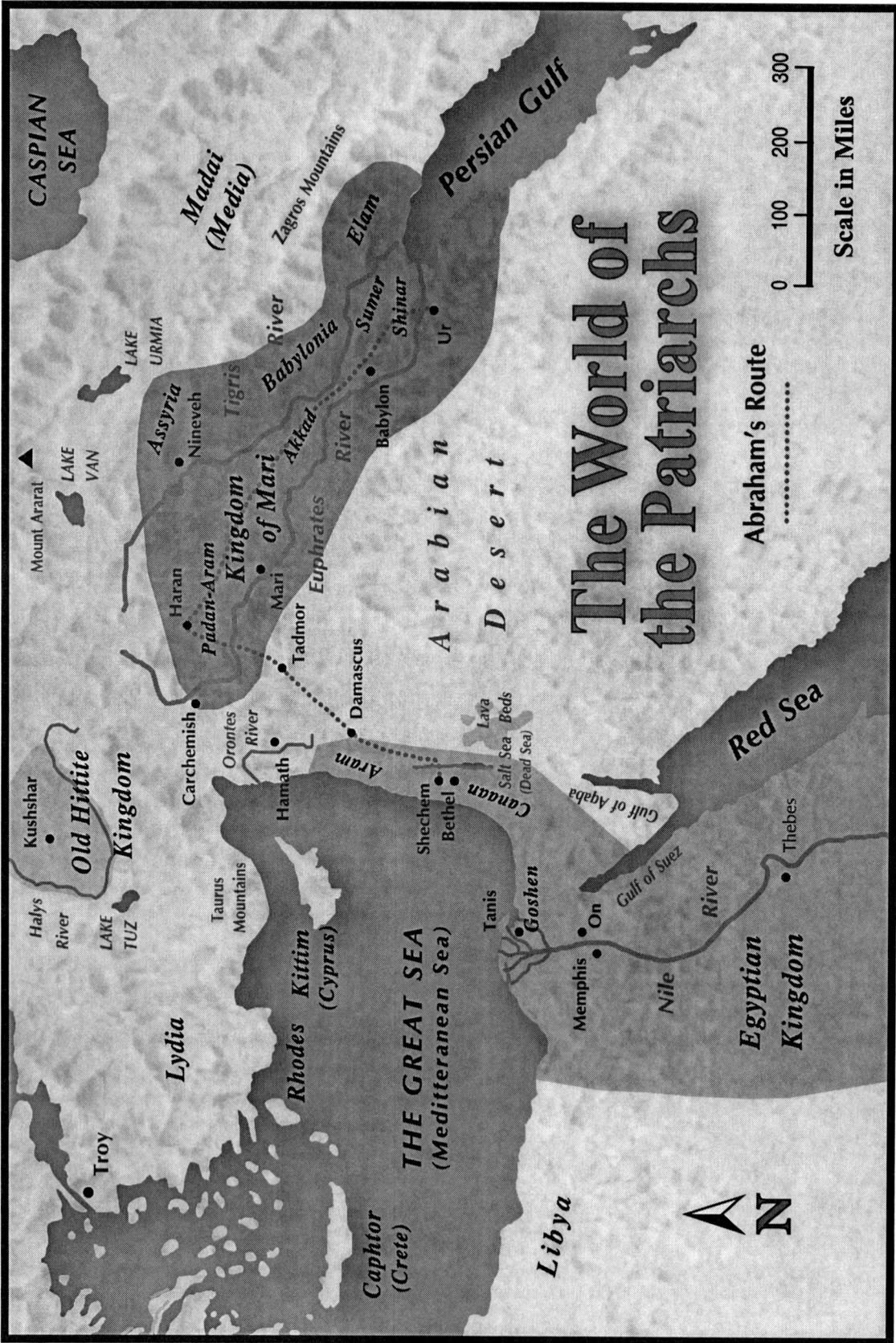

The World of
the Patriarchs

Abraham's Route

•••••••

CASPIAN
SEA

*Madai
(Media)*

LAKE
URMIA

Zagros Mountains

Elam

Persian Gulf

River

Babylonia

Sumer

Shinar

Tigris

Assyria
• Nineveh

Akkad

• Babylon

Ur •

*Kingdom
of Mari*

River

Mount Ararat ▲

LAKE
VAN

Haran •
Padan-Aram

Mari •

Euphrates

Tadmor •

Damascus •

A r a b i a n

D e s e r t

Carchemish •

Kushshar •

*Old Hittite
Kingdom*

Taurus
Mountains

Orontes
River

Hamath •

Aram

Shechem •
Bethel •

Canaan

Lava
Beds

Salt Sea
(Dead Sea)

Gulf of Aqaba

Red Sea

Halys
River

LAKE
TUZ

Lydia

Rhodes

*Kittim
(Cyprus)*

*THE GREAT SEA
(Mediterranean Sea)*

Tanis •

Goshen •
On •

Gulf of Suez

Nile
River

Thebes •

Troy •

*Caphtor
(Crete)*

Libya

Memphis •

*Egyptian
Kingdom*

N

Scale in Miles

0   100   200   300

MAP TWO

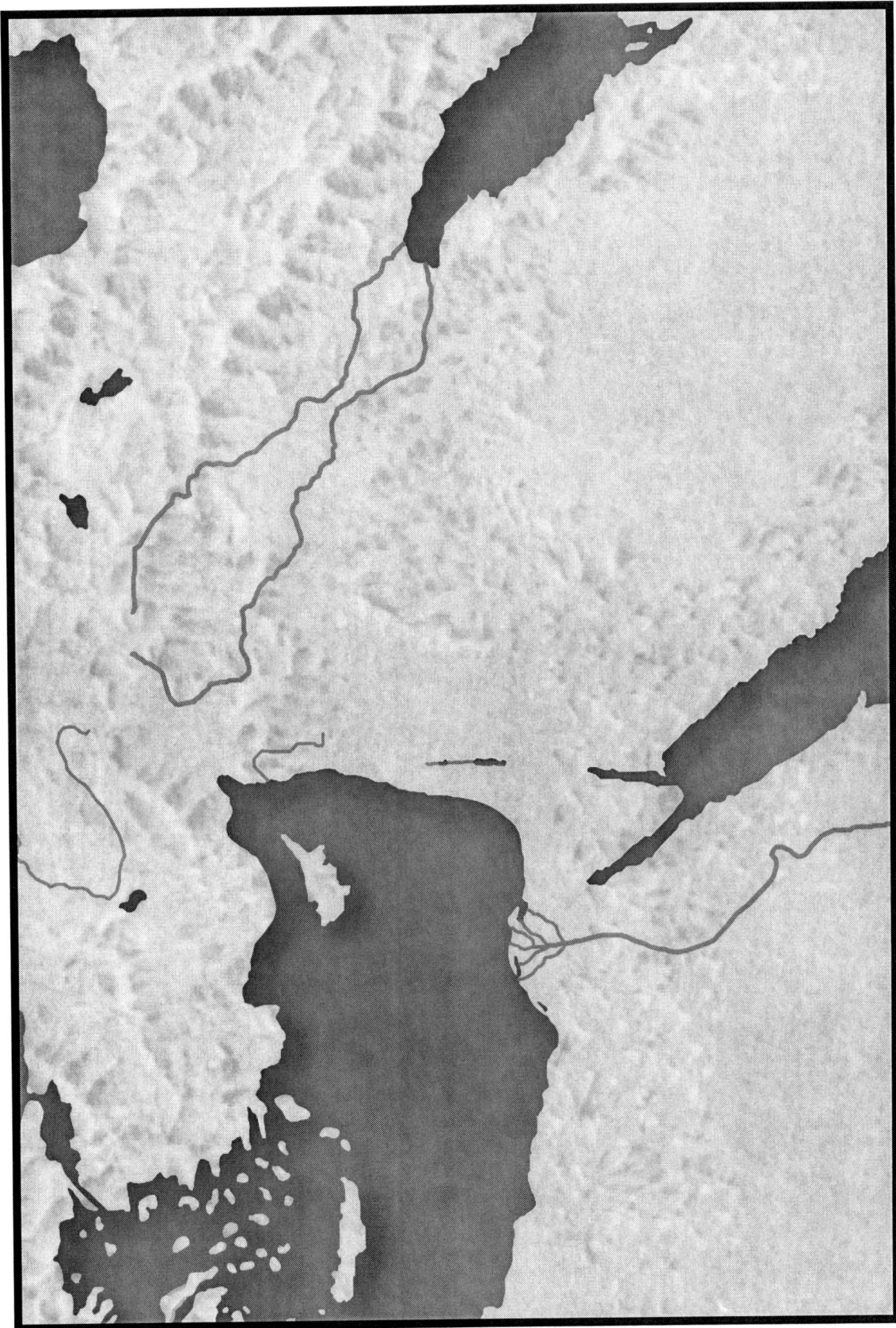

The text here in Genesis sounds as if Abram received his call to leave his family and country in Haran, yet God reminded Abram that He brought him out of Ur (15:7). Abraham himself said that it was God who took him from the land of his nativity (24:7). In the New Testament, Stephen is specific in saying, "God appeared unto our father Abraham, when he was in Mesopotamia, before he dwelt in Haran" and told him to leave. "Then came he out of the land of the Chaldeans and dwelt in Haran" (Acts 7:2-4).

Though Nahor is not mentioned as moving with the rest of the family, he either moved at this time, and is not mentioned in this short synopsis, or he came a little later. When Abraham sent his servant for a wife for Isaac, the servant went to "the city of Nahor" (Gen. 24:10) where he found Bethuel, the son of Nahor, living with his children, Laban and Rebekah. This place in turn is called Paddan-aram (28:2,5) and Haran (28:10; 29:4), so the term "city of Nahor" seems to have been used to mean the "home of Nahor, "which was by then the city of Haran.

Chronology Note

Stephen says that when Terah was dead, God brought Abraham from Haran to Canaan (Acts 7:4). Since Terah was 205 years old when he died (Gen. 11:32), and Abram was 75 years old when he left Haran (12:4), then Abram was born when Terah was 130 years old. Terah began begetting his children at the age of 70 (11:26). Since Abram is mentioned first in the list of Terah's children, we tend to think that he was the firstborn, but then the chronology does not fit the other passages given about their ages at various points in the story. Abram's name is listed first because he is the primary character whose story the writer follows.

It is only a coincidence that the name of this city where the family lived for a time is the same as the name of the dead son of Terah. The city of Haran was already an important trading post along the heavily traveled trade routes.

In leaving Ur of the Chaldees, Abram and his family left one of the largest, most progressive cities of the ancient world Extensive excavations have been done there, and it is evident they had an elaborate system of writing, advanced means of mathematical calculations, religious records, refined specimens of art, a school system, and many other things man finds necessary for civilization.

If it is true that Ur was a prosperous city as archaeologists tell us it was, then how could Abram leave a settled, likely comfortable culture, to become a nomad, to go to a place very different to the one he knew? The writer of Hebrews gives the answer (Heb. 11:8-10, 13-16—NASV): 15 By _faith_ Abraham, when he was called, obeyed... By _faith_ he lived as an alien in the land of promise as in a foreign land... for he was looking for the city which has foundations, whose architect and builder is God "Why did he obey? How could he leave his home and family? Because he had full trust in the One who told him to go! He was confident he could rely upon God to fulfill every promise He had made. Furthermore, he knew that this world was not his final home. It did not matter which city or which land he lived in upon this earth, because his destination was a city built by God Himself, an eternal home. This example is one of the many reasons why Abraham is called the father (the prototype) of all who believe (see Rom. 4:11, 16; Gal. 3:6-8, 26-29). Let us learn and apply the lesson of deep faith and trust as we spend our lives in service to God Let us follow Him during the difficult times as well as during the easy times.

Abram moves to Canaan (12:1-9):

Now the Lord had spoken to Abram, saying, "Get out of your country, from your relatives, and from your father's house to go to the land that I will show you. I will make of you a great nation, and I will bless you and make your name great, and you will be a blessing. I will bless those who bless you and curse those who curse you, and in you shall all families of the earth be blessed."

Abram did as God said and left Haran, taking his wife, his nephew Lot, all their possessions, and all their servants that they had acquired in Haran. Abram was 75 years old. They came into the land of Canaan and set up camp at Shechem where Abram built an altar and worshiped God. There God appeared to Abram and said, "I will give this land unto your descendants."

From Shechem, Abram moved southward to a place between Bethel and Ai, and he built an altar there. He continued moving south until he was in the Negeb *(the South—KJV).*

The city of Harran in modern Iraq, site of ancient Haran.

Add these promises from God to Abram in 12:1-3, 7 to the one God made to Eve in Genesis 3:15. We will see these promises fulfilled in the unfolding of the scheme of redemption—in the revealing of God's plan for the salvation of mankind There are six elements to the promises given in these verses:

- *Abram's descendants will become a great nation.*

- *Abram himself will be blessed materially and spiritually.*

- *His name will be exalted*

- *He will be a medium of blessing to others.*

- *Through his seed all families of the earth will be blessed.*

- *His descendants will receive the land of Canaan.*

The promises that Abram would be blessed personally, and that his name would be exalted, were for his personal benefit. Verse 3 explains that other men would be blessed or cursed depending upon their attitude toward Abram. Then he is promised that all people will be blessed through his seed. For the purpose of watching the scheme of re-

Promises to Abraham:

**Land
Nation
Spiritual**

demption unfold, let us resolve these verses into three major promises, which we shall term:

- *The great nation promise,*

- *The spiritual blessing promise (through his seed all would be blessed),*

- *The land promise.*

The rest of the Bible is the story of the fulfilling of these three promises. Therefore, be sure you know what promises were made to Abram, and be sure to watch for the fulfillment of each promise as you continue studying Bible history.

Notice some specific points about these promises:

- *Most of us will never have a separate, distinct nation of people that will come from us, nor will our descendants inherit a particular land to become the home of our nation. This was one of the main reasons God chose to separate Abram from his relatives—so that his family could develop into a distinct nation, not just as a branch of a much larger group. God had a plan for this distinct nation that would come from Abraham.*

- *So far, God has unfolded only a little part of His plan for the redemption of mankind: A descendant of Eve will come who will triumph over Satan (3:15); He will come through Abraham and He will bless all families of the earth (12:3). Paul makes the point in Galatians 3:16 that this promise to Abraham about all families of the earth being blessed through his seed referred to one particular seed—that is, one particular descendant—that the word was singular as God spoke to Abraham. Therefore, God promised that He would bless all nations through a particular descendant* of Abraham (the Christ), not just through the Jews that would come from him.

The Hebrew writer says that Abraham went out, not knowing where he was going (Heb. 11:8), not knowing his final destination. In Genesis 11:31 and in 12:5, the text says the family went out "to go into the land of Canaan." These passages leave us with two possibilities:

- One, the family left Ur, not knowing they were going to Canaan and were told sometime afterward, in which case it was the historian's observation that they left Ur to go to Canaan.

- Two, they knew they were going to Canaan, but did not know that it would be their final destination until Abram arrived in the land and was told by God that it would be the land God would give to his descendants.

- The outcome is the same in either case: the immediate family lived in Ur, they left there at God's command, and their God-given destination was the land of Canaan.

Though we are not told Abram's exact route, he probably traveled south on the King's Highway from Haran, because it was already a prominent caravan route from Paddan-aram to Canaan. As the company approached the land, almost certainly they went down the valley of the Jabbok River, crossed the Jordan, and ascended into the hill country by way of the Wadi-Farah. (A wadi is a water course that runs only in wet weather) This ravine or canyon opens out onto the ridge of the hill country near Shechem. This seems to be the logical route because Shechem is the first camping place mentioned in the land.

Take careful notice that Abram's first order of business in a new place was to build an altar to worship God. God was number one with Abram.

The Negeb was an arid region between Beersheba and Kadesh-barnea. It was relatively fertile during the rainy season, but dry as a desert during the rest of the year. From Beersheba, a trade route called the Way of Shur went out into the Wilderness of Shur and on to Egypt. Beersheba was not yet a city, and there is no information given about exactly where Abram camped in the Negeb at this time.

Abram lies to Pharaoh (12:10-20):

A famine arose in Canaan, and Abram went into Egypt to escape its effects.

Abram's wife Sarai was very beautiful. Therefore, he made an agreement with her when they left his father's house that wherever they went she would say, "He is my brother" (see 20:13-14), because Abram feared that someone, seeing her beauty, would desire to have her and might kill him in order to get her. As they approached Egypt, he said, "Please say that you are my sister, so that things will be all right with me where you are concerned."

When they arrived in Egypt, the Egyptians did notice Sarai's beauty and told Pharaoh about her. When Pharaoh learned she was Abram's sister, he took her to be one of his wives. Pharaoh gave Abram sheep, oxen, male and female donkeys, men-servants, maid-servants, and camels—a very great gift. But God brought some form of severe distress upon Pharaoh and all his household because of Sarai.

Pharaoh called Abram to him and said, "Why have you done this thing to me? Why did you not tell me she was your wife? Why did you say she was your sister, knowing that I would take her to be my wife?

Map Assignment:

Draw and label Abram's route from Ur to Haran, and then on to Shechem in the land of Canaan on your blank map. You need to become very familiar with this map of Bible lands because it will be used frequently throughout the Old Testament.

Take her and leave my country." Pharaoh ordered his men to escort Abram and his family out of Egypt.

A famine in Abram's promised land did not diminish his appreciation for the land. Every land has its years of drought and years of plenty.

Obviously God communicated with Pharaoh in some way to let him know that the distress that was upon his household was a direct result of his taking Sarai rather than an unfortunate coincidence. The historian gives us no information about how Pharaoh learned the cause of the trouble.

have been able to see a large portion of the land of Canaan. Lot saw before him all the valley of the Jordan, and especially the part that lay to the south. There the plain was well-watered. Before God destroyed Sodom and Gomorrah, it was like the garden of Jehovah. Acting selfishly, because the land he chose was the greenest available, Lot chose the fertile plain of the Jordan and separated himself from his uncle. Abram continued to live in the hill country of Canaan, and Lot moved his tents toward Sodom, where the people were sinners against the Lord in the extreme.

When Lot was gone, God said to Abram, "Look all around you, because this is the land which I will give to you and to your seed indefinitely, and I will make your descendants like the dust of the earth. Get up and walk throughout the land." So Abram arose and traveled southward again until he came to the oaks of Mamre which were at Hebron.

Map Assignment:

Continue following Abram's route. Draw it from Canaan to Egypt and then back to Canaan. Notice how far he has traveled from Ur by this time—a total of about 1500 miles—in a day when travel was very slow and difficult.

Abram and Lot separate (13:1-18):

Abram returned to the Negeb with Sarai and his nephew Lot. Continuing northward he came to the altar he had built near Bethel and Ai, and he worshiped the Lord.

Abram was very rich, not only in silver and gold, but also in cattle. Lot was rich also. Together they had so many herds and flocks there was not enough grass and water in any one spot to supply their needs. Soon their herdsmen were quarreling over provisions for the animals.

Finally, Abram took his nephew aside and said, "Look, we are brethren. Let there be no strife between me and you, between my herdsmen and yours. Isn't the whole land before us? Go where you will. If you go to the right, I will go to the left, or if you go left, I will go right."

Lot scanned the horizon, and standing on the hill country between Bethel and Ai, they would

Notice that God repeats the land promise and the nation promise to Abram this time. The spiritual promise is not included on this occasion. Stay alert to which promise

Promises under Consideration:

**Nation
Land**

is under consideration in each passage where one is mentioned. It makes a difference in understanding the passage.

The locations of Sodom and Gomorrah have never been definitely identified, but it now seems evident they were in the area beneath the shallow part of

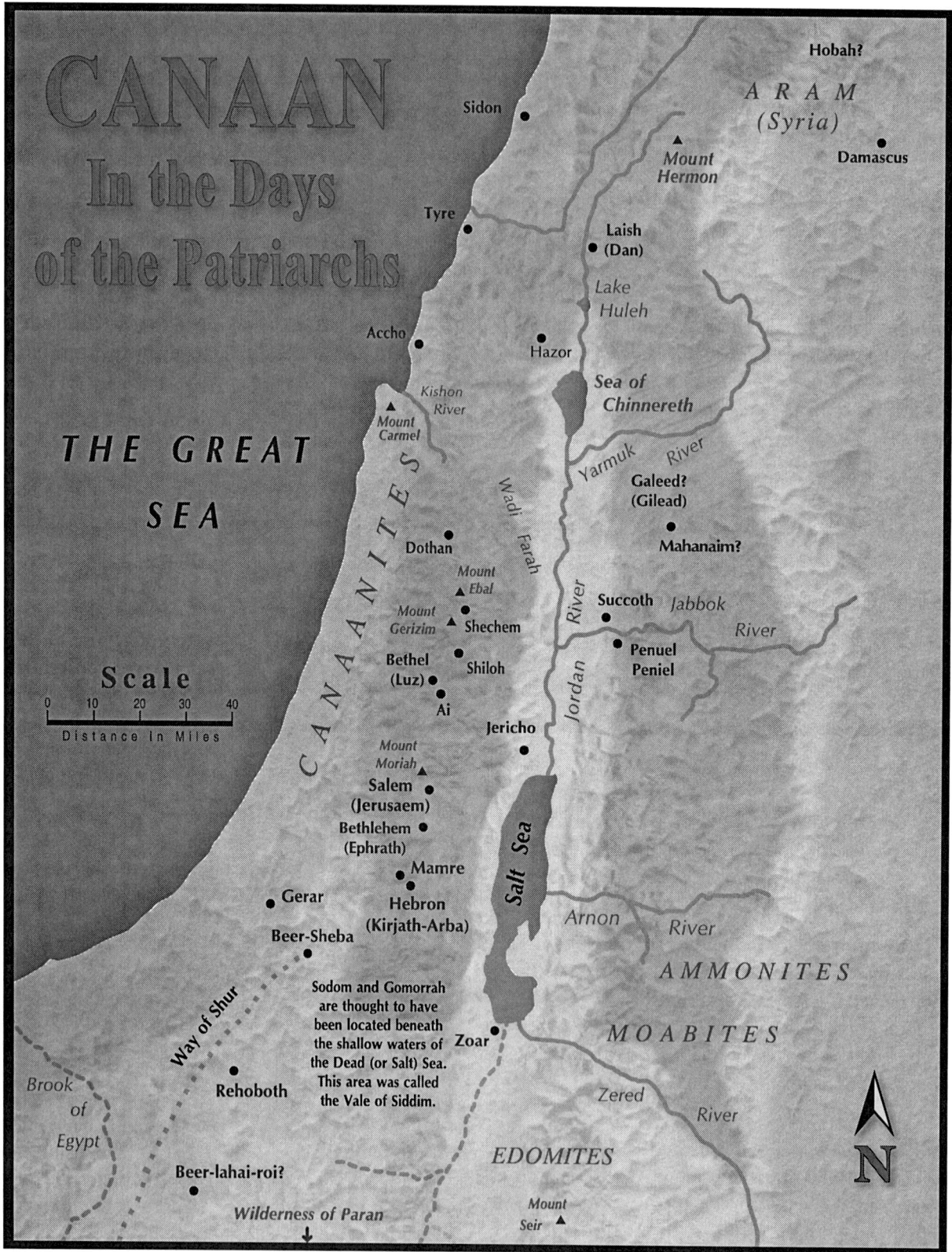

CANAAN
In the Days
of the Patriarchs

Hobah?

ARAM
(Syria)

Sidon

Mount
Hermon

Damascus

Tyre

Laish
(Dan)

Lake
Huleh

Accho

Hazor

Sea of
Chinnereth

Kishon
River

Mount
Carmel

THE GREAT
SEA

Yarmuk   River

Galeed?
(Gilead)

Mahanaim?

Dothan

Mount
Ebal

Wadi Farah

Mount
Gerizim

Shechem

Succoth

Jabbok

River

Bethel
(Luz)

Shiloh

Penuel
Peniel

Scale

0   10   20   30   40
Distance In Miles

Ai

Jericho

Jordan River

Mount
Moriah

Salem
(Jerusaem)

Bethlehem
(Ephrath)

Salt Sea

Mamre

Gerar

Hebron
(Kirjath-Arba)

Arnon   River

Beer-Sheba

AMMONITES

Way of Shur

Sodom and Gomorrah
are thought to have
been located beneath
the shallow waters of
the Dead (or Salt) Sea.
This area was called
the Vale of Siddim.

Zoar

MOABITES

Brook
of
Egypt

Rehoboth

Zered   River

N

Beer-lahai-roi?

EDOMITES

Mount
Seir

Wilderness of Paran

MAP THREE

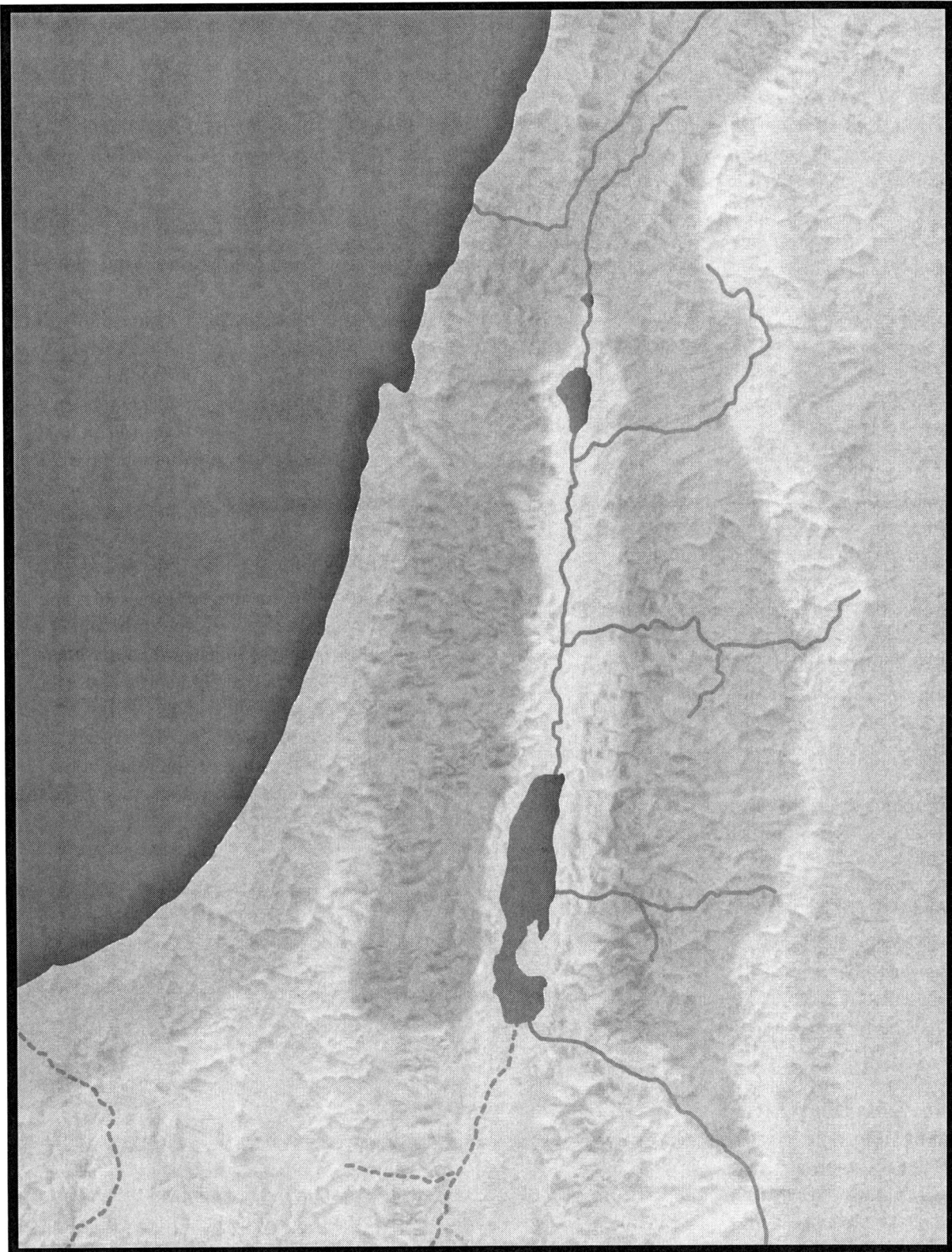

the Dead Sea in the south. *The entire region around the Dead Sea is barren today, and has been since the destruction of Sodom and Gomorrah—but note the specific description of its beauty here in Lot's day.*

but information such as the mention of Hebron's early name helps in approximating the date of Abraham's life. That puts the date for his story at about 2000 BC.

> *Map Assignment:*
>
> Look at the map of the land of Canaan and label the places on your blank map where Abram has camped so far—Shechem, Bethel and Ai, the Negeb, and now the oaks of Mamre near Hebron. Label Sodom and Gomorrah as Lot's home.

Abram rescues Lot (14:1-24):

Sometime after Lot moved into the plain of the Jordan, he found himself involved in a very dangerous political situation. Five cities of the plain, Sodom, Gomorrah, Admah, Zeboiim, and Bela (Zoar), were brought under the yoke of a coalition of kings of city-states located near the Tigris and Euphrates Rivers. These kings were Amraphel king of Shinar, Arioch king of Ellasar, Chedorlaomer king of Elam, and Tidal king of Goiim. These four kings held the five kings of the plain of the Salt *Sea (Dead Sea)* under oppression for twelve years. In the thirteenth year the kings of the valley of the Salt Sea revolted and provoked a response from the Mesopotamian kings the following year.

Hebron is one of the oldest cities in the world that is still in existence. It was built seven years before Zoan (later Tanis) in Egypt (Num. 13:22). Its early name was Kiriath-arba (Josh. 14:15; 15:13). Since Zoan was founded as the capital for the Egyptian rulers of the twelfth dynasty (2050-1800 BC), it was built around 2050, with Hebron begun seven years earlier. Estimates of Abraham's date vary from 2090 to 1875 BC. The references to Hebron in Abraham's life indicate it was still a relatively young city at that time. In this passage, he has moved to "The oaks of Mamre, which are in Hebron" (13: 18). Mamre was the name of another wealthy chieftain similar to Abram. This description indicates the area was better known by its association with Mamre than it was by the name of the city. Several years later, Sarah died "in Kiriath-arba (the same is Hebron)" (23:2), another indication that the time was early in the city's history. If Hebron were built around 2050 BC, then Abraham was there sometime later—but how much later is uncertain. It is impossible to arrive at an exact date,

> *Map Assignment:*
>
> Look on your study map of Bible Lands to see where these invaders came from, then label these places on your blank map. Look on your map of Canaan and see the locations of the oppressed cities and label them on your map of Canaan.

Chedorlaomer king of Elam was the leader of the invading army. Leading the forces with him, he came down the east side of the Jordan, smiting the enemy as they met each one. They fought the Rephaim *(giants, or long-stretched ones)* in Ashteroth-karnaim *(later the capital of Og king of*

Bashan, Deut. 1:4). They destroyed the Zuzim, the Emim, and the Horites, and then swung around to the south to Enmishpat *(well of judgment)* which is Kadesh-barnea.

Here, the combined forces of the five kings of the south went out to fight the kings of Mesopotamia. Slime *(tar)* pits abounded in the valley of the Salt Sea. *(The area referred to is in the southern part of what is now the Dead Sea.)* There the kings of Sodom and Gomorrah fled and fell *(died).* The other kings of the plain and their forces escaped into the mountains. The invaders sacked the cities of Sodom and Gomorrah, and among their captives, they took Lot and his possessions and departed.

One man managed to escape and made his way to the oaks of Mamre where Abram was living. Abram had made a mutual defense agreement with three chieftains who lived in the vicinity—Mamre, Aner, and Eshcol. When Abram heard that his relative Lot had been taken captive, he led forth 318 of his own men trained in the use of weapons. Verse 24 tells that his three confederates and their men joined the effort also. They pursued the kings of Mesopotamia to Dan.

Having caught up with the invading force, Abram divided his men, attacked by night, and chased them to Hobah north of Damascus. He regained all the spoil, Lot with his possessions, and the rest of the people.

On their way home, they crossed the Jordan and traveled toward the city of Salem *(later to be called Jerusalem).* The king of Sodom *(successor to the one that fell),* and the kings that were with him, went out to meet Abram in the valley of Shaveh which is the King's Vale *(or dale).*

Melchizedek, king of Salem, also met them with provisions of bread and wine. He was priest of God Most High, and he blessed Abram saying, "Blessed

The modern city of Hebron.

is Abram of the Most High God, Founder of heaven and earth, and blessed be God Most High who has delivered your enemies into your hand." At this Abram gave Melchizedek a tenth of the spoil, thus acknowledging his priesthood to be genuine.

The king of Sodom said to Abram, "Give me the people you have rescued, and you keep the goods."

But Abram replied, "I have sworn to Jehovah, God Most High, Maker of heaven and earth, that I will not take even the smallest thing from this spoil, lest you say, 'I have made Abram rich.' The only thing I want is the expenses of my men and the portion belonging to Aner, Eshcol, and Mamre who went with me."

Judging from the people they fought along their way, the invaders came down the King's Highway as they entered the land Almost certainly they returned the same way, because that was their most logical way home. Often in the book of Genesis, a name is used for a town before that name was actually given. For example, we learn later that the place Moses is already calling Bethel was called Luz until Jacob renamed it Bethel (28:19.) So we usually interpret this mention of Dan as the city of Dan located in the foothills of Mount Hermon, the common Dan in Israelite history after the days of the Judges (see Judg.

18). But this time seems to be an exception to the rule for identifying a place by its later name. If Dan is a reference to old Laish, then there are some surprising features about this narrative. The well-known city of Dan was not called that before or during the days of Moses, so he would not have used that name. Laish/Dan was somewhat remote, so it seems unlikely that the kings of Mesopotamia would have gone there on their way home. Neither was Laish/Dan the only city by that name. There is a Dan mentioned in Deuteronomy 34:1 that was in the northern part of Gilead on the eastern side of the Jordan. The same Dan may be mentioned again in 2 Samuel 24:6. This Dan on the east side of the Jordan, somewhere in northern Gilead, is much more likely the one referred to here because it would have been on or near the trade route as the kings headed north on the King's Highway.

Map Assignment:

Find the well-known city of Dan on your map of Canaan and then see how a less well-known one in Gilead would seem to fit the narrative better. The outcome of the story is the same, no matter which Dan it was.

Notice that each little city mentioned had its own king at this early point in history. These cities with their kings were called city-states. The whole territories of Mesopotamia and Canaan were dotted with city-states, while Egypt already had a united government. The kings of these small city-states controlled their own city, plus whatever villages or other cities they were strong enough to take. So even though there were several kings and several little city-states involved in this conflict, we must not interpret the story in terms of our modern warfare. Obviously, by forming a coalition of city-states, the kings of Mesopotamia had created a strength that enabled them to oppress city-states far from their homeland This coalition from Mesopotamia was

probably trying to hold control of the trade route that went down the eastern plateau of the Jordan (the King's Highway).

Melchizedek is not a supernatural figure, and there is nothing mysterious about his story. The historical record tells us no more about him than is recorded here. The writer of Hebrews uses the example of Melchizedek to teach some lessons about Christ (see Hebrews 7):

- His title "Melchizedek" means king of righteousness.

- Salem means peace, so by being king of Salem he was "king of peace."

- Melchizedek was not priest because he was of a certain lineage, but because he was specially appointed to the position.

- Abraham acknowledged the priesthood of Melchizedek by giving him a tithe of all, and, when Abraham paid tithes to Melchizedek, Levi did also because he was a descendant of Abraham (he was "still in the loins of his father, "Heb. 7:9-10).

- Melchizedek was greater than Abraham because the greater always blesses the lesser, and Melchizedek blessed Abraham.

- Thus Melchizedek becomes a figure of the Christ.

God's covenant with Abram (15:1-21):

Some time passed, and God spoke to Abram in a vision, saying, "Do not fear, Abram, because I am your shield, and your exceeding great reward."

Abram trusted God, but he was very concerned about a problem which he saw as an obstacle to God's fulfilling His promises, so he said, "O Lord Jehovah, what do you plan to do, seeing that I have no child? It looks as though my heir will be my steward, Eliezer of Damascus. You have given me no seed, and one associated with my house will be my heir."

Jehovah replied, "This man will not be your heir, but one who will come from your own body will be your heir." God brought Abram outside and said, "Look at the heavens and count the stars if you can. This is how many your seed will be."

Abram believed God and it was counted to him for righteousness.

God said, "I am Jehovah who brought you out of Ur of the Chaldees to give you this land for an inheritance."

Abram asked, "How can I be sure I will inherit it?" (*This question was a request for a confirmation of the promise.*)

God said, "Take for me a heifer three years old, a she-goat three years old, a ram three years old, a turtledove and a young pigeon."

Abram did as God had said, splitting the larger animals and laying them with each half corresponding to its mate and the birds lying whole across from each other. When vultures would have descended upon the carcasses, Abram drove them away.

As the sun was setting, a deep sleep fell upon Abram, plus a great dread and darkness. Then God said, "Know without doubt that your descendants will dwell in a land which is not theirs and will serve the people there, and they will afflict your descendants for 400 years. Then I will judge that nation whom they serve, and afterward they will come out with abundant possessions. But you will die in peace and will be buried in a good old age. Then in the fourth generation your seed will come here again. It is not the time for them to inherit the land now because the wickedness of the Amorites is not yet filled full." When it was dark God passed between the pieces of the animals in the form of a furnace (*the Hebrew word means a stove or cylindrical fire-pot*) and a flaming torch.

Thus, in that day, God entered into a covenant with Abram, saying, "To your descendants I have given this land, from the river of Egypt (*the brook of Egypt on the southern edge of Canaan, not the Nile*) to the great river, the river Euphrates." This was the land which in Abram's day belonged to the various tribes of Canaan.

The verse in this chapter concerning Abram's faith (15:6) is quoted in Romans 4:3, in Galatians 3:6, and in James 2:23. In the first two references the point is that Abraham was righteous because he believed God, not because he was perfect in his works (his obedience). The third reference, however, shows that it was not by his faith alone that he was saved, but by his faith as it prompted him to obey the instructions of God. We will say more about the use of the passage in James when we get to chapter 22 of Genesis.

The particular promise under consideration as Abram's faith is described concerns the great nation that was to come through him (15:1-6). Look at the question, at God's answer, and then at Abram's faith. Abram has said, "I have no son; how can there be a nation through me?" God replies, "You will have a son; your descendants will be as numerous as the stars." And Abram firmly believed what God said. His faith concerning this promise never wavered again. Notice that God specified here that the child would be Abram's, but He did not specify that it would also be Sarai's.

Verses 7-21 repeat the land promise. Abram asks God to confirm His promise by giving him a distinct sign. God did not rebuke Abram for asking for confirmation, so God did not consider his request unreasonable. The account that follows is the sign that God gave to make that original promise into a binding covenant with Abram.

Promises under Consideration:

Nation
Land

This way of making a covenant was prevalent among many ancient nations. The Hebrew words translated "Make a covenant," mean literally "to cut a covenant," referring to the cutting of the animals. The word for covenant, "berith," comes from a word which means "to eat" and reflects the practice of the parties to a covenant eating together after passing between the cut pieces of the animal(s). This method is alluded to by Jeremiah in the case of Israel at Mount Sinai (Jer. 34:18). Here in Abram's day, the normal pattern of both passing between the pieces was not followed, because only God did so. This difference is because, although there were two parties, as in all covenants, in this covenant that God was making, Abram did not stand on an equality with God. God extends the agreement to man as a benefit of His grace.

The period of 400 years in 15:13 is best taken as a round number consisting of four generations of a hundred years each (15:16). The "fourth generation" is also somewhat figurative because there is a wide variation in how many generations were in Egypt from family to family. There were only four generations listed in the tribe of Levi to Moses (Exod. 6:16-20), but six from Joseph to Zelophehad, six from Judah to Nahshon, seven from Judah to Bezaleel, and nine or ten from Joseph to Joshua.

The figure of 430 years is the literal number given for the sojourn in Egypt in Exodus 12:40. In Galatians 3:17 Paul follows the LXX which takes the words, "Now the time that the children of Israel dwelt in Egypt was four hundred and thirty years," and translates them: "Now the time that the children of Israel dwelt in the land of Egypt and in the land of Canaan was four hundred and thirty years." This translation was traditional in the synagogues, and since the exact figure did not matter to Paul's argument, he used the traditional words without comment.

We will see this prophecy about Abram's descendants fulfilled in every detail:

- They will dwell in a land not their own where they will be oppressed.

- The oppressors will be punished by God.

- His people will come out of that land with great possessions.

- They will make their way to the land of Canaan and inherit it as their own.

Begin strengthening your own faith, and the faith of those you teach, by seeing that when God makes a promise—whether for blessing or for punishment—He always keeps that promise.

Birth of Ishmael (16:1-16):

Sarai had an Egyptian handmaid named Hagar; and since she herself remained barren, Sarai suggested to Abram: "Look, Jehovah has kept me from bearing a child. Let me persuade you to go in unto my handmaid. Perhaps I can provide an heir through her."

It had been ten years since Abram had entered the land of promise, so he agreed to Sarai's suggestion and took Hagar for his concubine. Soon Hagar conceived, and when she saw that she was to have her master's child, she had only contempt for her mistress Sarai.

Sarai went to Abram and said, "My wrong is upon you. I gave my handmaid into your arms, and when she saw that she had conceived, she had nothing but contempt for me. May Jehovah judge between me and you."

Abram did not attempt to uphold Hagar's status as a wife on a par with Sarai, but said, "Look, your maid is yours to deal with however you see fit." But when Sarai began to exert her power over her handmaid, Hagar fled.

Hagar was on her way to Shur when the angel of Jehovah found her by a fountain of water. He asked her, "Where have you come from, and where are you going?"

Hagar answered, "I am running away from my mistress Sarai."

The angel told her: "Go back to your mistress and submit to her hand." Then the angel continued with a promise about her child: "I will greatly multiply your descendants so that they cannot be counted. You will bear a son, and you will call his name Ishmael (God hears) because the Lord has heard your affliction. He shall be as a wild donkey among men; he will live in a state of perpetual feuding and will live to the east of his brethren."

Hagar called the name of Jehovah that spoke unto her, saying, "Thou art El Roi *(the God of seeing)*, because in this very place I have looked upon Him who sees me." Therefore the fountain was called Beer-la-hai-roi *(the well of the Living One who sees)*.

At the appropriate time, Hagar bore a son, and Abram named the child Ishmael. Abram was 86 years old when the child was born.

Sarai's recommendation was not as unusual, or inappropriate, in that day as it would be in our day. It was a day of multiple wives, or as this would be—a wife, plus a concubine. If the wife could not have children, this was a common way of providing an heir. A concubine was a wife—not a part of an adulterous relationship—but she did not have the social standing of the primary wife. She had no authority in the family or in household affairs. Her children could be sent away with a small present from the father, or they could inherit on an equal basis with the sons of the wife (or wives), depending upon the decision of their father.

Though the description of the nation to come through Ishmael might be considered an unusual one for the promised nation through Abram, Hagar was still told there would be a nation through him, and he was Abram's son. Abram and Sarai thought their problem of an heir to inherit all of God's promises was solved. There was now a son of Abram to be the first of the great nation that would inherit the land of Canaan—but God did not need their help.

Covenant of circumcision (17:1-27):

When Abram was 99 years old, Jehovah appeared unto him and said, "I am God Almighty *(El Shaddai)*; walk before me and live blamelessly, and I will set my covenant between me and you, and I will multiply you exceedingly." Abram fell on his face before the Lord, and God talked with him, saying:

For my part, I hereby set my covenant in force with you, and you will be the father of a multitude of nations. In keeping with my promise, your name will no longer be Abram *(Ab=father + ram=exalted)*, but Abraham *(Ab=father + raham=-multitude)* because I have made you the father of many nations. I will make you exceedingly fruitful, and I will make nations of you, and kings will come from you. I will establish my covenant between me and you and your seed after you throughout their generations for an everlasting covenant, to be a God to you and to your seed after you. I will also give to you and to your seed after you the land where you have dwelt, all the land of Canaan, for an everlasting possession, and I will be their God.

On your part, you shall keep my covenant, you and your seed after you throughout their generations. The covenant to which I refer, which you will keep, is that every male among you will be circumcised in the flesh of his foreskin. Circumcision will be a symbol of the covenant between me and you. Every male among you will be circumcised the eighth day after birth: whether he is born in your house or bought as a servant, every male is to be circumcised. The sign of my agreement with you will be in your flesh for an everlasting covenant. The male who is not circumcised in

Middle-Eastern wild donkey.

the flesh of his foreskin shall be cut off from his people; he has broken my covenant.

God continued, "Your wife Sarai shall no longer be called Sarai *(princely?)*, but Sarah *(princess)*. I will bless her and give you a son by her. Yes, I will bless her and she will be the mother of nations; kings of peoples shall come from her."

At this, Abraham fell on his face, and laughed, saying to himself, "Shall a child be born to him that is a hundred years old? And shall Sarah, who is ninety years old, bear?"

Abraham pleaded with God: "Oh that Ishmael might live before you."

God answered: "No, Sarah your wife will bear you a son and you will call his name Isaac *(laughter)*. I will establish my covenant with him for an everlasting covenant for his seed after him. As for Ishmael, I have heard you. Behold, I have blessed him and will make him fruitful, and he will beget twelve princes, and I will make him a great nation, but I will establish my covenant with Isaac whom Sarah will bear to you at this appointed time next year." Then God ended His conversation with Abraham.

In keeping with God's commandment, Abraham was circumcised, and he had Ishmael and every male in his household circumcised. Abraham was 99 years old and Ishmael was 13.

Chronology Note

The text tells how old Ishmael was when he was circumcised, but we could have determined his age by the passages telling Abraham's age:

- *How old was Abraham when Ishmael was born (16:16)?*

- *How old was Abraham when he was circumcised (17:1, 24)?*

- *How long had Abraham been in the land when God commanded him to be circumcised (12:4)?*

All the names of God throughout the Bible make statements about His revealed role among men. So far we have had Elohim, the basic word for God the Creator, perhaps a term emphasizing strength. Then we had Jehovah God, Yahweh Elohim, emphasizing that this is the Manifested One, the One who reveals Himself to man. Melchizedek spoke of God Most High to emphasize His pre-eminence. Hagar called Him El Roi, the God who sees. And now God speaks of Himself as El Shaddai, God Almighty, that is, the One who is more than strong enough to do whatever it takes to accomplish His will, no matter how impossible it seems to men.

The two promises discussed in this chapter are the nation promise and the land promise. Circumcision is given here as a symbol, a sign that each male

Promises under Consideration:

Nation
Land

born or bought into the family was a part of the nation promised to Abraham, and as a part of that nation, an heir to the land that would be given. In the New Testament, there was great misunderstanding about the sign of circumcision, because the Jewish Christians thought that the Gentiles would have to be circumcised before they could be partakers of the blessings in Christ (see Acts 15). Their misunderstanding came because they thought only Jews could have blessings from God. Notice that the spiritual blessing was not included here in the discussion of Genesis 17 when the rite of circumcision was commanded. The spiritual blessing was separate, and would be offered to all mankind, not just to Abraham's fleshly descendants. In Galatians 3:6-14 Paul uses Genesis 15:6—"And Abraham believed in God, and it was reckoned unto him for righteousness"— to say that Abraham was not saved by circumcision nor by any work of the law of Moses. Therefore all, Jews and Gentiles, are justified by faith.

Paul uses this passage where Abram's name was changed to Abraham to say that he became the father of all who believe—including all of us who have become Christians. That blessing is the ultimate fulfillment of the promise that Abraham would be the father of many nations (see Rom. 4). Paul was not giving a new meaning to the Old Testament passage—rather he was explaining what God meant when He made the promise to Abraham.

The word "everlasting" in these verses is used to mean "eternal" by a variety of false teachers. Thus they say that by an eternal covenant the land of Canaan is to be an eternal possession of the Jews. But the word "olam," translated here as everlasting, and elsewhere as forever, does not necessarily mean eternal. For example, in Exodus 21:6, if a Hebrew servant elected to remain with his master after seven years of service, his master would bring him to the magistrates and pierce his ear with an awl, and he would serve him "forever" (olam). The word refers to an indefinite length of time ("a time hidden"). It can mean unlimited, eternal, but one must determine its meaning from the context. In no passage can the decision about whether its meaning is eternal or an indefinite period of time be settled by appealing to the intrinsic meaning of the word itself. The covenant of circumcision and the possession of the land by Abraham's descendants were to be for an indefinite period, but not without end, as the subsequent history of the Jews will show. God's promise about their retaining the land was based upon the faithfulness of the Israelites (e.g. see Deut.28:63-66; 29:22-28; and many other passages) .

Notice the words, "...to be a God unto thee, and to thy seed after thee," and "I will be their God" (Gen. 17:7-8). These are the words of the basic agreement between God and man throughout the ages. God wants, and has always wanted, to have a relationship with men whereby He can bless them and they, in turn,

will love Him and serve Him. This passage is the earliest occurrence of the expression. Remember this expression, for we will take note of it throughout the rest of the Bible story (see Rev. 21:3, 7).

The expression "cut off" is used often in the law of Moses to refer to the punishment for disobedience. In Leviticus 17:9-10, a distinction is made between the cutting off inflicted by men upon those who break the law and that which God will inflict. It seems evident that the "cutting off" was death rather than mere ostracism, because how would God ostracize someone from the people differently than the magistrates? There are some parallel passages where "cutting off" is used in one passage and "death" is used in the other (see Exod. 31:14-15; Lev. 20:2-3; 23:29-30; Num. 15:30-36). Therefore, "cutting off" as it is used here is probably the penalty of death, meaning that one who refused to be circumcised was to be counted as rebellious against God and was to be punished by death (see Exod. 4:24-26).

God did not rebuke Abraham for his laughter as He later rebuked Sarah (18:13-15). Paul says that Abraham did not stagger at the promise of God through unbelief (Rom. 4:18-21). We must, therefore, understand that Abraham's laughter was not the laughter of cynical doubt, but that of delighted amazement. Notice that it is here that the name Laughter (Isaac) is given for the child, just as we might name a child Joy in our day.

Abraham was asking more than that Ishmael would be blessed because that request was granted, but God's reply was, "No." Abraham was asking that God let Ishmael be his heir—to be the one through whom the promises concerning the nation and the land could be fulfilled

The Lord visits Abraham (18:1-15):

One day as Abraham was sitting in the door of his tent in the heat of the day, he looked up and saw three men standing a little way off.

> **Genesis 17:7-8: "I will establish My covenant between Me and you and your descendants... to be God to you and to your descendants after you... and I will be their God."**

Promptly he ran to them and bowed himself low and said, "My Lord, if I have found favor in your sight, do not go by me. Let a little water be brought, and wash your feet and rest under the tree. I will get you some bread to eat, and when you are refreshed, then you can go on your way."

The men agreed, saying, "Very well."

Abraham hurried into the tent and told Sarah, "Quickly, prepare three-fifths of a bushel of fine meal and knead it and make cakes." Then he ran to the herd and selected a young, tender calf and gave it to a servant who hurried to dress it. He also took butter and milk and set them with the meat before his guests. Then Abraham stood by them under the tree as they ate.

The three men said, "Where is Sarah your wife?"

"She is in the tent," Abraham replied.

The leader of the three said, "I will surely come back this time next year, and your wife Sarah will have a son."

Sarah, who was in the door of the tent behind the men, laughed to herself. Sarah knew she had always been barren and now she was no longer young enough to have a baby. She thought in her heart, "Now that I am old, shall I have pleasure, I and my lord who is also very old?"

Jehovah asked Abraham, "Why did Sarah laugh asking, 'Shall I indeed bear a child?' Is anything too hard for Jehovah? This time next year Sarah will have a son."

Sarah denied having laughed, but God said, "No. You did laugh."

Since Abraham addressed his guests as "My Lord" from the first moment, he may have guessed these were supernatural beings, but he may have used the term "ny lord" the first time merely as an expression of respect to a stranger. This event is referred to by the Hebrew writer to make the point that we should be as hospitable as Abraham (Heb. 13:2). Abraham was gracious—though probably not yet realizing these were more than ordinary men. Because he was so hospitable, he succeeded in entertaining the Lord and two

angels. In verse 3, Abraham used the Hebrew word for lord that could refer to God or to a person of honor. By verse 13, however, the word translated as Lord in the KJV is the word for Jehovah. Only God could predict a child would be born to Sarah.

Sarah's laughter, unlike Abraham's (17:17), was the expression of doubt, not delighted astonishment. That doubt had to be overcome because it would be by her faith that she would receive power to conceive (Heb. 11:11).

Cakes of bread in that day were usually relatively flat, round loaves of unleavened bread baked on hot stones. Calves were usually roasted on a spit over an open fire. Whether it was cut into small portions on occasions such as this in order to speed the cooking is impossible to know. Unless the milk was fresh, it was usually served curdled to preserve it.

Abraham pleads for Sodom (18:16-33):

After eating, Abraham's visitors arose and looked toward Sodom. Abraham walked with them a little way, and Jehovah said, "Shall I hide from Abraham what I am about to do, seeing that he will become a great nation and that all nations will be blessed through him? For I have chosen him so that he may command his children after him to keep the way of the Lord, to do righteousness and justice so that Jehovah can fulfill His promise which He has spoken to Abraham."

Then Jehovah said, "The cry of Sodom and Gomorrah is great, and their sin is dreadful. I will go now and investigate and see whether they have done according to what I have heard. If not, I will know." The other two visitors *(angels, 19:1)* went on toward Sodom while Jehovah still stood with Abraham. Abraham came near to Him and said, "Will you consume the righteous with the wicked? Suppose you find fifty righteous people in the city, will you go ahead and destroy it and the righteous who are within? That is not at all like you, to slay the righteous with the wicked, to treat them both the same way. That is totally unlike you. Surely the Judge of the whole earth will do right."

Jehovah answered, "If I find in Sodom fifty righteous people, I will spare the whole place for their sake."

Abraham said, "Look at me, nothing but dust and ashes, and yet I have ventured to speak unto the Lord!

Suppose the fifty righteous lack five; will you destroy the city for the lack of five?"

God answered, "I will not destroy the city if I find forty-five."

Abraham continued, "What if you find forty?"

"I will not destroy the city for the sake of forty."

"Please do not be angry, and I will speak: suppose you find only thirty?"

God answered, "I will not do it if I find thirty there."

"What if you find only twenty?"

"I will not destroy the city for the twenty's sake."

Finally Abraham said, "Do not be angry, and I will ask once more: suppose you find only ten?"

God said, "I will not destroy it even if I find only ten." Then Jehovah went on His way, and Abraham returned to his tent.

God, of course, could know without going into Sodom and Gomorrah what their wickedness was. God accommodates Himself to men in language like this and in deeds such as these, so that we can better understand His workings and decisions.

One of the most common features of successful intercession in the Bible is supplication which appeals to the character of God for its basis.

Destruction of Sodom and Gomorrah (19:1-29):

At evening the two angels reached Sodom where they were seen by Lot as he was sitting in the gate.

He went to them, bowed low, and said, "Sirs, please plan to stay with me in my house tonight. Then in the morning you can get up early and be on your way."

But the angels said, "No, we will remain in the street tonight."

Lot urged them the more to stay with him. Finally, they consented and went into his house where he baked unleavened bread and made a feast for them.

While Lot was entertaining his guests, the men of Sodom, both young and old, from every corner of the city, came to Lot's house. Calling out to Lot, they said, "Where are those men who came in to you tonight? Bring them out to us so that we can molest (*sodomize*) them."

Lot went out of the door and closed it after him. He said, "I beg of you, brothers, do not behave so wickedly. Look, I have two virgin daughters. Let me bring them out to you, and you can do whatever you want to them, but do not molest these men because they have come under the shadow of my roof."

The people cried out, "Get back," (*or 'Get out of our way'*) and then to one another they said, "This fellow came in, a foreigner, and already he plans to be our judge. Now we will deal worse with you than with them." And they pressed forward toward Lot to break the door down.

At that point the angels reached out, and, seizing Lot, they pulled him into the house and shut the door. They struck the men outside with blindness so that they exhausted themselves trying to find the door.

The angels said to Lot, "Have you any relatives here other than those in this house: a son-in-

Sodom and Gomorrah once stood within the barren land somewhere near the Dead (or Salt) Sea.

law, sons, daughters, or anyone else? Go get them quickly because we are about to destroy this place, because their outcry, the wickedness of the people, has come to be great before the Lord. He has sent us to destroy the city."

So Lot ran out and spoke to his sons-in-law, saying, "Quick, get up! You must leave because Jehovah is about to destroy this city." But his sons-in-law did not take his warning seriously. They thought he was joking.

When morning came the angels hurried Lot, telling him, "Get up. Take your wife and your two daughters that are here and leave before you are consumed in the punishment of the city."

As Lot continued to linger, the angels took his hand, the hand of his wife, and of his two daughters, and brought them out of the city. They said, "Run for your life! Do not look behind you and do not stay in the plain. Escape to the mountains or you will be destroyed."

Lot pleaded with them: "Please don't make me flee to the mountains. I have found favor in your sight, and you have shown me great mercy, but I cannot flee to the mountains lest calamity overtake me before I get there. Look, this city is nearby. I could flee to it. It is a little city. Please let me escape there. Is it not just a small city? There I can live."

The angels answered, "See, I grant you this wish also; I will leave this city you have mentioned. Hurry now and go there because I cannot do a thing until you are there." Therefore the name of the city was called Zoar (Little). Zoar was formerly called Bela (14:8).

The sun was fully up when Lot arrived in Zoar. Then God caused burning brimstone to rain upon Sodom and Gomorrah from heaven. All the cities of the plain, their inhabitants, and even the vegetation, were all destroyed.

During the flight of Lot, his wife looked back and she was turned into a column of salt.

Early that morning while the devastation was occurring, Abraham went to the place where he had stood before the Lord and looked toward Sodom and Gomorrah and all the plain. Everywhere thick smoke billowed up from the land like the smoke of a furnace. But in the midst of all the destruction, God remembered Abraham and spared Lot from judgment (2 Pet. 2:6-9).

Lot's invitation to the angels to come into his house was a hospitable one, but their answer was appropriate according to the habits of travelers of that day. All travelers went prepared to spend their nights camped out in the streets of a city or in the fields along their way.

The homosexuality of the people of Sodom was utterly shameless and unrestrained. They were willing to break even the most ancient rules regarding hospitality. The term "sodomy" for homosexuality comes from the wickedness of this ancient city. If sodomy were such an abomination to God in that day, can it be thought to be any more pleasing to Him today?

When Lot offered his daughters to the mob it was a heinous thing to do. It illustrates, however, that to him, the requirements of hospitality ranked higher than the safety and well-being of one's own family. Also, it shows that Lot did not consider rape to be the abomination that sodomy was.

Brimstone is sulphur. The substance was either hot ash or molten lava. At the time of this sulphurous rain, the Dead Sea was formed. It is likely that the northern part of the Dead Sea was already there, and that the southern shallow part of the Sea now covers the cities of the plain. The full extent of the effects of this destruction is not given, but the description of the plains of the Jordan found in 13:10 is very different from the description of the area around the Dead Sea throughout the rest of the Bible and from its description today. The whole area was barren and desolate after this event.

Why was Lot's wife turned into a column of salt? It is enough that she looked back when the angels said do not do so. The angels almost certainly meant do not stop to watch the destruction. It may have been a regretful looking back—a longing for what was back there. Jesus' use of this example in Luke 17:32 seems to support this thought. All we know for sure is that she looked back when she had been forbidden to do so.

Lot and his daughters (19:30-38):

Lot was afraid to remain in Zoar, so he went up into the mountains with his two daughters and lived in a cave. After a time, the oldest daughter said to her sister, "Our father is old, and there is no man available to be our husband. Let us make our father drunk, and we will have children by him so that his line will be continued."

Therefore they made Lot so drunk he did not know when his oldest daughter went in and went to bed with him or when she left. The next day she told her sister, "Look, last night I lay with my father. Let's make him drunk tonight also, and you go in and go to bed with him, and thus we will preserve our father's lineage." So that night the younger daughter went in to Lot, and he did not know when she came in or when she left.

Both of the daughters of Lot thus conceived by their own father. The older gave birth to a son whom she called Moab, who became the father of the Moabites. The younger gave birth to a son whom she called Ben-ammi. He became the father of the Ammonites.

The Moabites settled in the mountains east of the Dead Sea and south of the Arnon River (Judg. 11:18). The Ammonites moved into the area just north of the Arnon River, but at some time before the Israelites invaded Canaan, the Ammonites were driven out of

their territory into the edge of the desert. By the time the Israelites came to the land, the territory just east of the Jordan and north of the Arnon was under the control of Sihon king of the Amorites (see Judg. 11:20-22).

Map Assignment:

Look on your map and see where the Moabites and Ammonites settled. Remember their origin and their location. We will meet these small nations many times.

Add the newest names to the family tree:

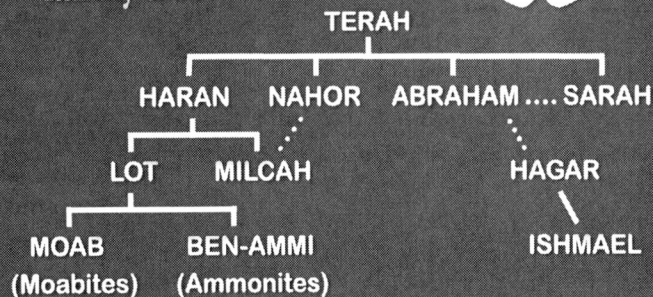

TERAH

HARAN — NAHOR — ABRAHAM .... SARAH

LOT — MILCAH — HAGAR

MOAB (Moabites) — BEN-AMMI (Ammonites) — ISHMAEL

Abraham lies to Abimelech (20:1-18):

Leaving the oaks of Mamre, Abraham traveled to the land of the Negeb *(the South)* and dwelt in the city of Gerar. Abraham arrived in Gerar with the story: "Sarah is my sister." So Abimelech *(a title meaning either "father of a king," or "my father is king"— probably the latter)* sent and took Sarah into his harem.

God spoke to Abimelech in a dream, saying, "Look, you are one step from being a dead man because of this woman you have taken. She is another man's wife."

Abimelech had not touched Sarah, and he said, "Lord *(not Jehovah, but the Hebrew word "Adonai," a term of reverence, but not a personal name of God)*, will you slay a righteous nation? Did not the man himself tell me, 'She is my sister'? And she, the woman herself, said, 'He is my brother.' In all honesty and with the most honorable intentions have I done this."

God replied, "Yes, I know, and I have also acted to hold you back from sinning against me. Therefore, restore the man's wife because he is a prophet. He will pray for you, and you will live. If you do not restore her, you and all that are with you will die."

Abimelech arose early the next morning and called all his servants together to tell them the information he had learned. Then he called Abraham to him and said, "What have you done to us? How have I sinned against you to make you cause me and my people to sin such a great sin? You have done things to me that ought not to be done. What possessed you to do such a thing?"

Abraham answered, "It was because I thought that surely the fear of God is not in this place, and they will kill me for my wife's sake. Besides, she really is my sister, the daughter of my father, but not of my mother, and she became my wife. When God caused me to wander from my father's house, I asked her to agree that everywhere we went she would do me the favor of saying of me, 'He is my brother.'"

Abimelech restored Sarah to Abraham along with a gift of sheep, oxen, and servants. He said, "Look, my land is before you: stay wherever you please." Then to Sarah he said, "See, I have given your brother a thousand pieces of silver to make things right between us."

Then Abraham prayed to God, and God healed Abimelech and his wife and his maid servants *(concubines)* so that they could bear children. For God had closed all the wombs of the household of Abimelech because he had taken Sarah, the wife of Abraham.

Map Assignment:
Gerar was located on a wadi called Jurf el Gerar. It was a city of the Philistines. See the note about the Philistines in Genesis 10:14. Label Gerar on your map.

In the similar story involving Pharaoh, the beauty of Sarah played an important role (12: 11-15). Here nothing is said of her beauty. Sarah was in her 90th year. Some have speculated that Sarah was rejuvenated in connection with her pregnancy, but there is no evidence for this. Sarah lived to be 127 years old (23:1), so her ninety years would not be the same as a ninety year old lady of today, but she probably was past the age when physical beauty would have captivated Abimelech. Probably Abimelech took her for his wife in order to make an alliance with the very wealthy chieftain Abraham.

Whatever was wrong with Abimelech and his household seems to have been something which prevented conception (or begetting) by obstructing the sexual act itself. Otherwise it would not have served to prevent Abimelech from touching Sarah sexually, and God said He held him back from sinning against Sarah.

Birth of Isaac (21:1-7):
Jehovah's prediction came true: He did unto Sarah as He had promised, and she conceived and delivered to Abraham a son in his old age at the very time God had set. Abraham called his son Isaac. When the baby was eight days old, Abraham circumcised him as God had commanded. Abraham was 100 years old.

Sarah said, "God has made me laugh; everyone who hears of this will laugh with me. Who would ever have told Abraham that Sarah would give children suck? I have given him a child in his old age."

It was truly a time of joy, and the child's name reflects that joy.

Chronology Note

How old was Abraham when Isaac was born?

How old was Sarah when he was born (17:17)?

How long had they been in the land of Canaan (12:4)?

How old was Ishmael when Isaac was born (16:16)?

Ishmael is sent away (21:8-21):

When Isaac was weaned, Abraham made a great feast. During the feast Sarah saw Ishmael mocking Isaac, so she said to Abraham, "Cast out this female slave and her son, because the son of a slave is not going to be heir with my son Isaac!"

Abraham was seriously disturbed over Sarah's request, but God said, "Do not worry about the lad and his mother. Do as Sarah says because it is through Isaac that your descendants will come. But I will also make a nation of Ishmael because he is your descendant."

Early the next morning Abraham got up and prepared bread and water for them, and then he sent Hagar and Ishmael away. Hagar and her teenage son *(he would have been at least fifteen or sixteen years old)* headed south into the wilderness of Beersheba. After a while the water was gone, and Hagar had Ishmael lie down under the shade of a bush. She moved away from him a few dozen yards and sat down because she could not bear to watch him die, and she wept aloud.

Then the angel of God called to Hagar from heaven and said, "What is the matter, Hagar? Do not

be afraid, because God has heard the voice of the lad. Get up, help the boy up, and hold him with your hand, because I am going to make him a great nation."

God opened Hagar's eyes so that she could see a well of water. She took the skin, filled it with water, and gave it to Ishmael to drink. God was with Ishmael so that he survived and became an archer in the wilderness of Paran. Hagar got a wife for him out of the land of Egypt.

What Sarah asked Abraham to do was against the laws and customs of the day. This is no doubt one of the reasons Abraham was so distressed over what Sarah said. Even though he was not a citizen of any government at the time, he still came from a society where laws existed saying that if a man had a son by a slave to be his heir, and then his own wife had a son, the son of the slave could not be disinherited. God, however, intervened to tell Abraham to do as Sarah had said.

This scene of Hagar's grief was compounded by a combination of physical need and of discouragement. Even though the region south of Beersheba is very dry during most of the year, it is possible to find water, if one knows where. But think of Hagar's position. For years now she had lived comfortably within Abraham's household, and she had even given her master a son. Ever since his birth it had been understood that her son would inherit all the vast wealth of Abraham—until this new child Isaac was born. Even after Isaac's birth, Hagar and Ishmael would have assumed that he would still inherit a large portion of Abraham's wealth. Now they are sent away as if in disgrace. Their bottle of water was empty, and they had not found water in this barren region—and they were deeply discouraged

Of course, God's speaking to Hagar was a supernatural happening, and God was certainly capable of miraculously making a spring of water for them, but more probably God helped her find water that was already available. God's point was, "Hagar, you and your son will be fine. It will be possible for you to find the necessities you need I will be with you, and Ishmael will not only survive, there will be a whole tribe of people to come from him." Encouragement was what Hagar needed most at this moment. We will learn a little more about the Ishmaelites in Genesis 25.

Abimelech makes a covenant with Abraham (21:22-34):

Abimelech the king of Gerar and Phicol the captain of his host approached Abraham to ask him to enter into an agreement of peace and friendship. Abimelech said, "God is with you in all that you do. Now please swear to me that you will not deal falsely with me or with my descendants, but please show kindness to us as I have shown kindness to you."

Abraham agreed to make the covenant, but first there was a matter that needed to be settled between them. Abimelech's servants had violently taken a well away from Abraham.

Abimelech said, "I do not know who has done this. I did not even know it had happened; this is the first I have heard of it."

Abraham began selecting sheep and oxen to give to Abimelech to confirm their covenant, but he also selected seven ewe lambs and set them apart from the others.

Abimelech said, "What are these seven ewe lambs for?"

Abraham said, "You are to take these seven lambs as a witness that I have dug this well." Therefore he called the place Beersheba *(well of the seven)* because they both swore to the covenant there.

After the covenant was made, Abimelech and Phicol arose and returned to the land of the Philistines *(back to Gerar)*. Abraham planted a tamarisk tree in Beersheba, and there he called upon the name of Jehovah who is the Everlasting God. He

remained in Philistine territory *(here at Beersheba)* a long time.

Beersheba is usually defined as the "well of the oath," but that connotation is apparently reserved until Genesis 26:33 where the word "shibhah" (oath) is used. In this first time it is named in 21:31 the word Beersheba is from "Beer shebhah" (seven), from the seven ewe lambs which were presented to Abimelech, his acceptance of which served as his testimony that the well indeed belonged to Abraham.

Beersheba was on the southern edge of arable land, just before the semi-desert Negeb began. These seem to have been very good wells that Abraham dug. Isaac will also live in the area and will use these same wells. Since the area was dry, good water was of prime importance, so a city grew up around the wells. The city will become known as the southern-most city of Israelite territory throughout most of their history.

The last verse of chapter 21 says that Abraham stayed in Philistine territory for many days, yet the context indicates that he was at Beersheba, which means that the Philistines were in control of that particular area at this time. That is almost certainly why they wanted this covenant of peace with Abraham.

Map Assignment:

Label Gerar and Beersheba on your map. Show that the Philistines controlled that territory at this time.

Abraham offers Isaac (22:1-19):

An unstated period of time passed, and God determined to test Abraham. He called, "Abraham." Abraham replied, "Here I am."

Without preamble, God said, "Take your son, your only son, the one you love, that is, Isaac, and go to the land of Moriah. There I want you to offer him to me as a burnt offering on one of the mountains I will tell you about."

Early the next morning Abraham got up, saddled his donkey, and took two of his young men along with Isaac. He took wood for the burnt offering and set out to go to the place God had told him. On the third day, Abraham looked up and saw the place a long way off. He told his young men, "Stay here with the donkey, while the lad and I go yonder to worship. Afterwards we will return."

Abraham laid the wood for the burnt offering on Isaac's back, and taking the knife and the *fire (hot coals)* in his own hand, Abraham and his son Isaac went together to the place of sacrifice. As they walked, Isaac asked his father, "See, here is the fire and the wood, but where is the lamb for a burnt offering?"

What turmoil must have been in Abraham's heart, but he calmly answered, "God will provide Himself a sacrifice, my son."

Finally, they reached the spot God had told Abraham about, and Abraham built the altar, laid the wood upon it, and then bound Isaac and laid him upon the wood. He took the knife in his hand to slay his son. Just then the angel of Jehovah called to him out of heaven: "Abraham, Abraham."

"Here I am," he replied.

"Do not lay your hand upon the lad. Do nothing to him because now I know that you fear God, since you have not withheld your only son from me."

Abraham looked up, and there was a ram caught by his horns in a thicket. He went and got the ram and offered it for a burnt offering instead of his son. Therefore he called the name of the place Jehovah-Jireh *(Jehovah sees),* so men still say, "On the mountain where Jehovah appeared."

The angel of Jehovah spoke to Abraham again, saying, "By Myself I have sworn that because you have done this thing, and have not kept back even your only son, I will surely bless you and will multiply your seed as the stars of heaven and the sand of the seashore. Your descendant will possess the gate of his enemies *(be victorious)* and in your descendant all families of the earth will be blessed, because you have obeyed my voice."

Afterward, Abraham and Isaac returned to the young men, and together they returned to Beersheba.

The word for descendant (or seed) in verses 17 and 18 is singular. See the note about this same promise in 12:3—God was promising that through one particular descendant, the Christ, all families of the earth would be blessed. Which two of the three major promises to Abraham are stated again as God talks with Abraham on this occasion?

Promises under Consideration:

Nation
Spiritual

Abraham exercised faith in God numerous times throughout his life. He left Ur by faith when God called him (Heb. 11:8), and he sojourned in the land of Canaan by faith (Heb. 11:9). He believed God when He promised him descendants as numerous as the stars of heaven, though he did not yet have a son, and his wife was barren (Gen. 15:6). The promise that he would be the father of many nations and that the land would be given to his descendants demanded faith because the promises were given and repeated before Isaac was born (Gen. 17). The faith of Abraham was thus a constant thing which sustained him throughout his life. His faith in God's promises was ultimately faith in God Himself.

When Isaac was born, Abraham could see that God indeed had kept the first part of His promise. No longer did he have to believe in the promise of a son, he had the son himself. This was the son through whom God specifically said the promises would be fulfilled. Imagine, then, the perplexity of Abraham

Ruins of ancient Beersheba.

when God told him to offer the son of promise as a burnt offering. But, Abraham did not scream or protest. Instead, early the next morning he set out to do God's bidding.

As Abraham obeyed God in offering his son, his faith was put to the ultimate test. Only by that great faith could he do what God had commanded Abraham's faith moved him to reason (see Heb. 11:19):

- God has given me Isaac as the son He promised

- God has specified that He will fulfill His promises through Isaac.

- Now God has commanded me to kill Isaac.

- Yet God's promises will be fulfilled.

- Therefore God must be going to raise Isaac from the dead.

The tremendous manifestation of faith in this event moved James of the New Testament to say that it was at this point in Abraham's life that his faith in the promise of God, a faith that he had even before he had a son, was shown in its full strength and maturity (James 2:21-23). It took great faith to believe that God would fulfill His promise through Abraham's son when there was no son, but how much more faith was required for Abraham to believe

that God would still fulfill His promises through a son who had been offered as a burnt offering! Faith without works is dead, being alone (James 2:17). This episode was a demonstration of the depth of Abraham's faith, but it also demonstrated his reverence for God and his willingness to obey God—even when he did not understand why the command was given. Therefore the angel of Jehovah said, "Now I know you fear God." Faith can be held in the heart, but it must lead one to bring forth obedience to God's laws before it is of value. God required Abraham to offer Isaac as a test of his devotion to God, to see by his actions whether he would choose God or his son if he had to make the choice. Abraham made the correct choice when the test was put before him.

One point that is not stressed in the Bible record is that Isaac had to be willing to submit to this action also. We are not told his age or his father's age at the time of this event, but Abraham was already an old man when Isaac was born. By now Isaac was old enough to carry a load of wood large enough to burn an animal up a mountain, so he was more than a mere child. If he were very old, he would have been strong enough to resist Abraham if he had chosen to do so, but there is no indication at all that he struggled when he learned of God's instructions or his father's intentions.

Though Abraham had sons by his concubines, God's terminology was correct when He spoke of Isaac as Abraham's only son. Isaac was the only son of Abraham's wife—and therefore, he was the only one recognized as the heir. He was the promised son.

The Hebrew word transliterated "Jireh" is a word that means to see, to appear, be seen. "It also means to see after, to provide." When Abraham said in 22:8 that the Lord will provide, he used this verb. Footnotes in various. Bibles vary in saying either "the Lord sees," or "the Lord provides" to interpret the name Abraham gave to the location. In this passage, the best sense is probably the idea of "provide," since there is no emphasis on a visual appearance of God to Abraham. Instead, the text says the angel of Jehovah spoke to Abraham "out of heaven."

The word "Moriah" is from the same word which is translated "to see." It means literally "shown of Jehovah," or "manifestation of Jehovah." It is applied to the mountain in Jerusalem where Solomon built the temple (2 Chron. 3:1). Possibly, therefore, the two Moriahs are the same, but that cannot be proven. First, Moriah in Genesis 22 is the land of Moriah, in which there would be a mount that God would point out as the location for the sacrifice. Second, the reason for calling the temple mount Moriah had nothing to do with Abraham, but rather with the appearance of Jehovah to David at the threshing floor of Araunah (2 Chron. 3:1; 2 Sam. 24:16-17). The two Moriahs may well be the same, but we have no actual evidence that they are.

The Hebrew writer refers to this occasion when God said, "By Myself have I sworn," to make the point that God swore by Himself because there was none greater by whom He could swear. God swore by the fact that He is God, that He is the ultimate source of all blessings, with the ultimate power to bring whatever He has promised to pass. The Hebrew writer uses the passage to assure the Jewish Christians (as well as all Christians since) that they could place the same reliance upon God's promises that Abraham could. (See Hebrews 6:13 and its context)

News from Nahor's family (22:20-24):

After these things, Abraham received news about his brother's family: "Milcah has borne children to your brother Nahor." Eight sons of Milcah are named, and of these, the one we need to remember is Bethuel. Nahor's concubine had also borne children, and four sons are named. Bethuel, by now, has a daughter named Rebekah.

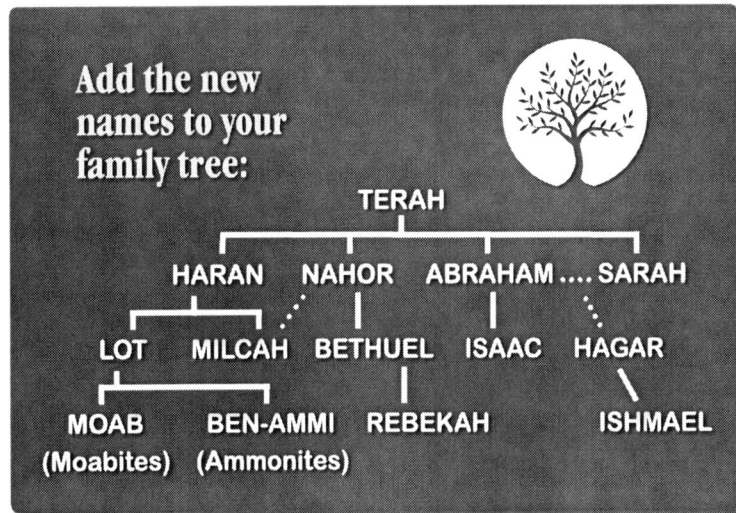

Add the new names to your family tree:

TERAH
├── HARAN ── NAHOR ── ABRAHAM .... SARAH
│   ├── LOT   MILCAH   BETHUEL   ISAAC   HAGAR
│   │   ├── MOAB   BEN-AMMI   REBEKAH   ISHMAEL
│   │   (Moabites) (Ammonites)

Chronology Note

Since Isaac was born when Abraham and Sarah were both old, his age fits with the age of Nahor's grandchildren.

Death of Sarah (23:1-20):

At the age of 127 Sarah died in Kiriath-arba (Hebron), and Abraham mourned and wept for her.

He came formally before the Hittite people to buy a burial ground. He said, "I am a stranger and a sojourner among you. I need to have in my possession a place where I can bury my dead."

The children of Heth (Hittites) answered, "Listen to us, my lord. You are a prince of God among us. In the best of our tombs you may bury your dead. None of us would turn you down."

Abraham bowed to the people and said, "If it is acceptable to you to let me have a burial place, then please ask Ephron the Hittite to sell me the cave of Machpelah which is in the end of his field. I will give him the full price for the cave for a burial place."

Now Ephron was sitting among his people, and he said where everyone could hear: "No, my lord, you do not need to pay me. I give you the field and

"Tomb of the Patriarchs," traditional location of the Cave of Machpelah.

the cave which is in it. In the presence of all my people I give it to you. Bury your dead."

Again Abraham bowed, and said, "If you will, I want to give you the price of the field so I can bury my dead."

Ephron answered, "My lord, listen to me: a piece of land worth 400 shekels of silver—what is that between us?"

So Abraham accepted Ephron's price and weighed out to him 400 shekels of silver before the people who were gathered there. The shekel was the standard weight used by merchants of that day.

Therefore the field of Ephron the Hittite, with the cave of Machpelah, was publicly recognized as now belonging to Abraham. Then Abraham buried his wife Sarah in the cave. The possession of the cave was guaranteed to Abraham by the children of Heth.

This little story gives an interesting glimpse into the way business was conducted in that day. Though this angle is of far less importance than the spiritual matters that take precedence throughout the Bible, it is interesting to notice these glimpses into the per-

sonal lives of the people as we travel through their history.

The Hittites were descendants of Heth, the second son of Canaan, the son of Ham, the son of Noah. (See Gen. 10:15; cf 26:34; 27:46.) Very early they established a strong kingdom around the Halys River in the area known as Asia Minor in the New Testament and as Turkey today. They had continual association and business relationships with the peoples of Egypt and Mesopotamia, which means they had continual associa- tion with the other Canaanite tribes who largely dwelt in the land of Canaan. There were several Hittite settlements in Canaan. Throughout the Old Testament the Hittites are listed as one of the prominent Canaanite tribes in the land. Through the years, there was frequent rivalry between Egypt and the Hittites over who would hold control over Ca- naan. Egypt held nominal control in Abraham's day, but it was called the "land of the Hittites" in Joshua's day (Josh. 1:4).

Remember the Cave of Machpelah. Sarah is the first to be buried there. Abraham, Rebekah, Isaac, Leah, and Jacob will all be buried there also.

Map Assignment:

Find the Halys River on Map #2 and see the location of the Hittite kingdom. Label the; river and the kingdom on your map.

Abraham gets a wife for Isaac (24:1-67):

Abraham was old and advanced in years and Jehovah had blessed him in everything. One day he called his chief servant to him, the one who was his steward and overseer, and said, "Please put your hand beneath my thigh. I put you under oath to Jehovah, the God of heaven and earth, that you will not take a wife for my son from the daughters of the Canaanites among whom I dwell. Instead you are to go to my country and to my relatives, and take from among them a wife for my son Isaac."

The servant said, "What if the woman is not willing to come with me to this land? Do you want me to take your son again into the land from which you came?"

Abraham answered, "You must be careful never to take my son back there. Jehovah, the God of heaven, the One who took me from my father's house and from my homeland, the same God who promised me saying, 'To your seed I will give this land,' He will send His angel before you, and you will be able to find a wife for my son from my people. But if the woman is not willing to follow you, then you will be free from your oath. You must not take my son there again." The servant swore to do as Abraham had said.

Taking ten camels and all sorts of goods belonging to Abraham, the servant departed and went to Mesopotamia (*Aram-naharaim, the land between the rivers*) to the city of Nahor (*the home of Nahor, not the name of the city*). He made the camels kneel down outside of the city by a well. It was evening, at the time when the women came out to draw water.

The servant prayed to Jehovah, "O Jehovah, the God of my master Abraham, grant me a favor and show kindness to my master Abraham. You see that I am standing by the fountain of water where the women come to draw water. Let it be that the maiden to whom I say, 'Give me a drink of water,' and she says, 'Drink, and I will draw for your camels also,'—let that be the woman you have chosen for your servant Isaac. In this way I will know that you have shown kindness to my master."

Even before the servant finished his prayer, Rebekah, the daughter of Bethuel, and the grand-daughter of Nahor and Milcah, came out with her pitcher on her shoulder. She was very beautiful and she was a virgin. She came to the fountain, filled her pitcher, and rose to leave. The servant said, "Let me drink a little water from your pitcher."

The maiden replied, "Drink, sir, and I will draw water for your camels also, until they have enough." Rebekah got busy drawing water and pouring it into the trough for the camels to drink. The servant stood watching, wondering at her, noting whether the Lord had made his journey prosperous or not.

When the camels finished drinking, the man gave Rebekah a golden ring (*a nose ring*) and two golden bracelets for her hands. He asked her, "Tell me, whose daughter are you? Is there room in your father's house for us to stay with you?"

She replied, "I am the daughter of Bethuel, the grand-daughter of Milcah and Nahor; and we have plenty of straw and food and room for you to stay."

When the servant heard this, he bowed low and worshiped Jehovah. He said, "Blessed be Jehovah, the God of my master Abraham. He has not forgotten to show mercy unto my master. He has led me to the house of my master's relatives."

Rebekah ran and told her mother's family what had happened. Her brother Laban ran out to the servant who was still at the fountain. Having seen the precious gifts the man had given to Rebekah, and having heard her story, Laban said, "Come in, you who are blessed of Jehovah. Why do you stand out here? I have prepared the house and also room for your camels."

Laban brought the party of men into the house. The steward unloaded the camels and saw that their needs were met, and then water was provided for him and the men who were with him to wash their feet. When food was set before them, the steward of Abraham said, "I will not eat until I have told you my errand."

Laban said, "Go ahead and tell us about it."

The steward said:

I am Abraham's servant, and Jehovah has blessed my master greatly. He has given him flocks and herds, silver and gold, many bond-servants, camels and donkeys. In her old age, Sarah, my master's wife, bore a son to my master. My master has given everything he has to that son.

My master made me swear that I would not take a wife for his son from among the Canaanites. He told me that Jehovah would send His angel before me so that I would be able to accomplish the task and find a wife from among his kindred. He said I would be clear of my oath if I came to his kindred and they would not let me have a wife for his son. And today, when I arrived, I prayed to Jehovah, the God of my master, and I asked Him to show me by a sign who the maiden was whom He had chosen for my master's son.

The servant continued his story to tell what had happened at the fountain, how Rebekah had been shown to be God's choice. He pointed out how remarkable it was for her to be so closely related to Abraham, and he gave glory to Jehovah for answering his prayer. Finally the servant said, "Now, if you will deal kindly and truly with my master, tell me, but if not, tell me, so that I can know which way to go next."

Laban and Bethuel replied, "The matter has come from Jehovah. It really is out of our hands. Here is Rebekah. Take her and let her be the wife of your master's son, as Jehovah has spoken."

Again, Abraham's servant worshiped God. He gave jewels of gold and clothes to Rebekah and precious things to her mother and to Laban. He and his men then ate and drank and spent the night.

The next morning, the servant arose requesting that he be permitted to return immediately to his master with Rebekah. Her brother and mother said, "Let the girl remain with us a few days, at least ten, and then she can go."

But the servant said, "Do not hinder me, seeing how Jehovah has made everything go well."

They called Rebekah to them and asked her, "Will you go with this man?"

She said, "Yes, I will go."

So her family sent away Rebekah, her nurse, and Abraham's servant, and his men to return to Abraham. They blessed Rebekah, saying, "May you, our sister, be the mother of thousands of ten thousands, and let your descendants hold their enemies under their power."

Rebekah and her maidens went with Abraham's servant, riding on camels, and they traveled all the way to the south of Canaan, to Beer-la-hai-roi which was in the Negeb. *(Remember that Hagar named Beer-la-hai-roi in Genesis 16. Look back to that story if you have forgotten the meaning of the name and why it was given.)*

Meanwhile Isaac had gone out in the evening to meditate. He looked up and saw the caravan coming. When Rebekah saw Isaac, she asked the steward, "Who is this man who is walking to meet us?"

"It is my master."

Hearing this, Rebekah took her veil and covered herself. The servant told Isaac all that had happened. So Isaac brought Rebekah to the tent of Sarah his mother, and she became his wife, and Isaac loved her. Thus Isaac was comforted after his mother's death.

This is a charming story. Imagine what it must have been like to be Rebekah—to have a stranger show up with a story about the uncle who moved away from the family so long ago; to learn that you have been selected by God to go as the wife of that uncle's son, and that the selection was made clear by the events at the well. No wonder she was willing to leave her own family and go to be part of that uncle's family! Not only is it a story of faith, it is the story of adventure and romance for Rebekah.

The test which Abraham's servant proposed was a good one. T. E. Lawrence (Lawrence of Arabia) writes in his book, The Seven Pillars of Wisdom, (p. 55) that when he lived among the Arabs, one time, after a mere day's journey, they watered their camels and the animals drank five gallons each. Since Abraham's servant had at least ten camels with him, at the minimum, Rebekah volunteered to draw fifty gallons of water! Not an impossible task, but certainly not the sort of task a girl would normally volunteer to do for a stranger.

Notice that the servant's name is not given in this story. Back in chapter 15, Abraham spoke of Eliezer as the steward of his house. This may have been the same man, but years have passed since chapter 15 and there is no way to know if Abraham's steward is the same.

Chronology Note

- How much older was Abraham than Sarah? (17:17)

- How old was Sarah when she died? (23:1)

- Therefore, how old was Abraham when she died?

- How old was Abraham when Isaac was born? (21:5)

- Therefore, how old was Isaac when his mother died?

- How old was Isaac when he married? (25:20)

- Therefore, how long was it after Sarah died before Abraham sent his servant to find a wife for Isaac?

Add Rebekah's brother Laban to your chart of the family tree:

Abraham and Keturah (25:1-6):

Abraham took another wife whose name was Keturah and she bore him six sons. Of these six, the one we need to remember is Midian. Isaac was Abraham's sole heir, but Abraham gave gifts *(probably generous ones)* to the sons of his concubines while he still lived, and he sent them away into the country to the east.

There is no way to know when Abraham took Keturah as a wife (or concubine). It is told here after Sarah's death, but it may be here because it is of lesser importance and was not told until now lest it interrupt the narrative of the main story line. As we will see in a moment, the writer of Genesis often tells of an event out of its chronological order so that it comes at a convenient point. In any account of history, two separate events may be happening simultaneously, but they can be reported only one at a time.

Consider for a moment: Abraham recognized that at 100 years of age, the chance of his having a son through purely physical processes was very slim (see Rom. 4:19). Think how much more unlikely it would be when he was 137 years old, the age he was when Sarah died, for him to marry a new wife and then have six sons by her. It is much more likely that this is a listing of the sons of another concubine of Abraham's, one that he had at the same time he had Sarah as his wife and Hagar as a concubine. The chapter tells of these sons and what became of them, of Abraham's death, and then it goes back to tell what became of Ishmael, the son of his other concubine Hagar. It fits together as a unit to finish the last details of Abraham's life.

Of these children of Keturah, the one we need to emphasize is Midian. He became the chief of the tribe that developed from all these sons. Midian 's descendants settled east of the Gulf of Aqaba and ranged north to areas east of the Dead Sea and the Jordan. They were a nomadic people, and at least one branch of them settled in the southern half of the Sinaitic peninsula. When Moses fled from Egypt he lived with a family of Midianites and married Zipporah, the daughter of Reuel (Jethro) who was priest of Midian (see Exod 2:1521; 3:1). The Midianites were enemies of the Israelites throughout most of their history. For example, the

Israelites will fight the Midianites near the end of their forty years in the wilderness (Num. 31) and again during the days of Gideon (Judg. 6-8).

The Midianites and the Ishmaelites joined forces and became one people, because the names are used interchangeably on more than one occasion. It was a caravan of Ishmaelites who approached the brothers of Joseph, with Midianite merchants in their midst. So Joseph was sold to Ishmaelites/Midianites. (See Gen. 37:25-28). The two names are used interchangeably again in the story of Gideon (see Judg. 6:1; 8:24).

Abraham's death (25:7-11):

Abraham lived to be 175 years old. When he died, Isaac and Ishmael buried him in the cave of Machpelah where Sarah was buried. Afterward God blessed Isaac, and he dwelt in Beer-la-hai-roi.

Chronology Note

Take a moment to look again at the chronology details given in the scriptures:

- How old was Abraham when Isaac was born (21:5)?

- How old was Isaac when he married (25:20)?

- How old was Isaac when his sons were born (25:26)?

- Therefore, how old was Abraham when Jacob and Esau were born?

- But how old was Abraham when he died (25:7)?

- Did Abraham live to see his grandsons?

- How old were they when he died?

This is one more example of how the writer tells an event out of its chronological order so that the main story is not interrupted. It seems that when Abraham sent his steward for a wife for Isaac, he was not only getting a companion for his son, he was establishing Isaac to become acting head of the family. The account tells the last details of Abraham's life and then immediately moves into the story of Isaac as head of the tribe that was developing.

Generations of Ishmael (25:12-18):

Ishmael was blessed by God, just as he had been promised. He had twelve sons and they lived in the Negeb and in the edge of the desert just as the sons of Keturah did. Ishmael died at the age of 137.

Look again at the family tree:

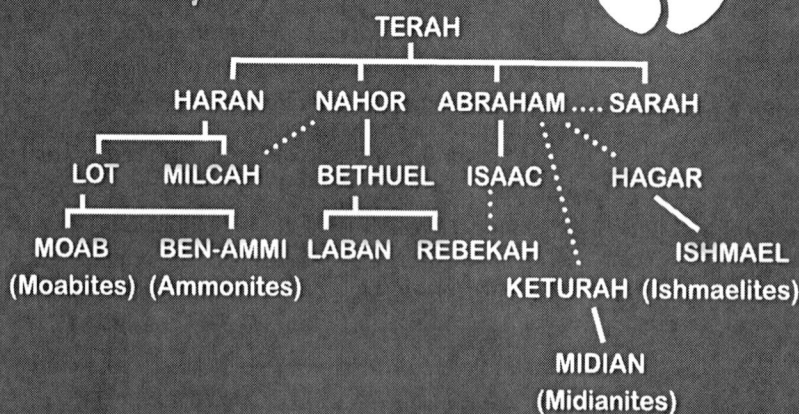

```
                        TERAH
         ┌───────────────┼───────────────┐
      HARAN           NAHOR        ABRAHAM .... SARAH
    ┌────┴────┐      ┌───┴───┐      ┌───┴───┐
   LOT     MILCAH  BETHUEL  ISAAC          HAGAR
  ┌──┴──┐          ┌───┴───┐
 MOAB  BEN-AMMI  LABAN  REBEKAH              ISHMAEL
(Moabites)(Ammonites)        KETURAH    (Ishmaelites)
                            MIDIAN
                          (Midianites)
```

Isaac
(Genesis 25:19-28:9; 35:28-29)

Moses begins the section starting in 25:19 with the expression, "And these are the generations of Isaac," just as he started the story of Terah and his family in 11:27: "Now these are the generations of Terah..." We are following the same pattern, but we making our headings in a way which we will be able to remember readily.

Most of the stories we have about Isaac are connected either with the story of Abraham or with Jacob. There is very little information about Isaac as the head of the family.

Birth of Jacob and Esau (25:19-26):

Isaac was forty years old when he married Rebekah. Years passed while Rebekah was unable to bear children, so Isaac prayed to God on her behalf. Jehovah heard his prayer and Rebekah conceived. As the babies grew within her, they struggled together, and caused Rebekah to wonder what the struggling meant. When she asked Jehovah about it, He told her, "Two nations are in your womb. Two peoples are going to be separated from your inward parts. One people will be stronger than the other, and the older will serve the younger."

When the babies were born, the first was covered with red hair, and they called his name Esau. Next came his brother, and his hand was holding Esau's heel, so they named him Jacob—which means, "supplanter," or "the one who takes by the heel."

Isaac was sixty years old when the sons were born.

The significance in the name Jacob or 'Supplanter" is one who takes the heel of another to pull him down in order to take his place.

Jacob buys Esau's birthright (25:27-34):

When the two boys were grown, Esau became a skillful hunter, a man of the field, but Jacob was a quiet man who preferred to stay in the tent. Isaac loved Esau because he ate his venison, and Rebekah loved Jacob.

One day when Esau came in from his hunt he was very hungry *(the original wording means starving for food)*. He found Jacob cooking some red lentil soup. He said to Jacob, "Feed me some of that *red* stuff you have there because I am weak." Therefore he was called Edom *(red)*.

Jacob said, "First sell me your birthright."

Esau answered, "I am about to die. What profit will the birthright do me then?"

But Jacob said, "Swear it to me first."

Esau swore and thus sold his birthright to Jacob. Then Jacob gave Esau bread and lentil soup, and after he had eaten and drunk, he arose and went his way. So Esau treated his birthright lightly.

The language describing the occupations of Jacob and Esau does not at all imply laziness on Jacob's part. He was a man who enjoyed the domestic side of life and did not care for the hunt. And it likely implies Jacob was more interested in what was happening in the affairs of the family and the work that was being done, since they were shepherds, not hunters, by trade.

Pay careful attention to the partiality the parents showed to each son. Esau was Isaac's favorite while Jacob was Rebekah's favorite. This partiality will pay a significant role in their story.

The Bible states that Esau "despised" his birthright and was, therefore, a profane man (Heb. 12:16). The word profane describes one who does not have a proper regard for things important. From the fact that later Esau was fully prepared to accept the blessing and portion of the firstborn (chap. 27), we infer that he did not take seriously this transaction with Jacob. Even so, Esau was treating what should have been a very, serious matter in a very unbecoming way. In a family such as this, the birthright would have made Esau head of the tribe as well as giving him the major portion of his father's wealth.

Jacob did not conduct himself righteously in this matter either because he should have been willing to feed a hungry brother. Nevertheless, in regard to the birthright itself Jacob was treating it with much more respect and desire for it than Esau did This is further indication that the expression that he was a man to dwell in the tent meant that he was the one concerned with the affairs of the property—and wanted to inherit the major portion of it.

Keep in mind that the birthright pertained to the inheritance of the firstborn, but not to the promises God had made to Abraham. When Jacob was given the inheritance which was to be the firstborn's, his father Isaac still recognized that only God could give the promises that had been given to Abraham (28:4).

Note the name Edom that was given to Esau here. His descendants will be called Edomites rather than "Esauites." Esau had red hair from the time of his birth, but the significance of the name meaning red came from this incident with the red soup rather than from the color of his hair.

Isaac's conflict with the Philistines (26:1-33):

A famine arose in the days of Isaac and he moved to Gerar in Philistine territory where Abimelech was king. Jehovah appeared to Isaac and said, "Do not go into Egypt; remain in this land and I will be with you and bless you, because I will give this land to you and to your descendants. I will also establish the oath I swore to Abraham your father, and I will multiply your descendants like the stars of heaven and will give them all these lands. And in your seed all the nations of the earth will be blessed. All this is because Abraham obeyed my voice and kept my commandments."

Promises repeated to Isaac:

Land
Nation
Spiritual

While Isaac lived at Gerar, the men asked him about his wife Rebekah. He answered, "She is my sister." He was afraid to tell them she was his wife because he was afraid they would kill him to get her, since she was beautiful. But one day, after Isaac had been there a long time, Abimelech looked out a window and saw Isaac playing with Rebekah in such a way that he knew she was his wife, not his sister. He called Isaac to him and said, "The truth is that this woman is your wife. Why did your say, 'She is my sister'?" Isaac answered, "Because I was afraid that I might be killed because of her."

Abimelech asked, "Did you think of the position you put us in? One of the people could easily have gone to bed with your wife, and you would have caused us to be guilty of a great wrong." The king then gave a command to all his people: "The one who touches this man or his wife shall surely be put to death."

The promises to Abraham have now been repeated to Isaac: nation, land, and spiritual. Notice also that God says that He is giving them to Isaac, because Abraham obeyed God This does not imply that Isaac

was wicked, but that Abraham's righteousness was bringing blessings upon the next generation.

The Hebrew word for sister was also used for close relatives in general, so Isaac's lie was parallel with Abraham's. It was not so much what Abraham and Isaac said in each case, but what they did not say. The wives were close relatives to their husbands, but that they were their wives was the most important fact to be told about them.

Notice that even a pagan king of the Philistines thought that it would be a great wrong if one of his men had taken Isaac's wife. The Philistines did not worship the true God—but they had a moral code in which fornication was considered a serious sin. And yet, in our modern world, fornication is considered the norm in the lives of most people! Do you think God considers it correct, normal behavior?

The name "Abimelech" seems to have been a title for the kings of Gerar rather than a personal name, so there is no way to know for sure whether this is the same Abimelech who took Sarah as a wife back in chapter 20. More than forty years have passed since then (because Isaac had not been born in chapter 20 and he was 40 by the time he married Rebekah, and this was sometime after that), so it is likely a different man. This king is at least more cautious than the Abimelech of the earlier story.

Isaac planted grain in the land and reaped a hundred-fold, and Jehovah blessed him. He grew more and more prosperous until he was very great, possessing flocks, and herds, and a great household. His prosperity provoked the envy of the Philistines.

Finally, Abimelech said to Isaac, "Go away from us because you are much mightier than we."

So Isaac left and dwelt in the valley of Gerar for a time. During the years since Abraham had been there and had dug wells, the Philistines had filled in the wells. Isaac gave orders for the wells to be dug again. One of the wells was an artesian spring. But when Isaac's servants cleaned the spring, the herdsmen of Gerar argued with Isaac's servants, saying, "This water is ours." Therefore Isaac called the well

Esek *(Contention).* He moved a little distance and his servants dug another well, and the Philistine herdsmen contended for it also, so he named it Sitnah *(Enmity).* Removing from Sitnah, they dug still another well, and the Philistines did not quarrel over it. Therefore, Isaac named it Rehoboth *(Room),* because he said, "Now Jehovah has made room for us, and we will do well in the land."

From Rehoboth he went up to Beer-sheba. That night Jehovah appeared to him and said, "Do not be afraid; I am the God of Abraham your father, and I am with you and will cause you to prosper for the sake of my servant Abraham." So Isaac pitched his tent at Beersheba and built an altar to God. He also instructed his servants to start digging a well.

Soon Abimelech came with his officers to see Isaac. Isaac greeted them with this question: "Why have you come to me, since you hate me and have driven me away from you?"

Abimelech said, "We have seen that Jehovah is with you, and we decided we need to have an agreement between us that you will do us no harm, just as we have not harmed you, but have sent you away in peace. You are now the blessed one of Jehovah."

The men made their agreement, swearing that they would do no harm to each other. When the Philistines left, Isaac's servants came to tell him that they had found water. He called the well Shibah *(Oath),* so the city is called Beersheba *(Well of the oath)* to this day.

It was at this same place that Abimelech and his officers made a similar covenant with Abraham (21:22‑32). It is likely a coincidence that both covenants were made at the same place, but this oath and the naming of the city re-affirmed the name it had been given in Abraham's day.

Abraham is never described as planting crops. Isaac, on the other hand, did so here in Philistine territory. Isaac used his inheritance wisely and made it prosper even more.

Map Assignment:

Note Isaac's peaceful nature. Rather than fighting the Philistines over rights to water, he calmly moved farther away from them. Find Gerar and Beersheba on your map. Esek, Sitnah, and Rehoboth were between these two places, but their exact location is not known, because cities did not grow up around these wells.

Esau marries Hittite women (26:34-35):

When Esau was forty years old, he married Judith, the daughter of Beeri the Hittite, and Basemath, the daughter of Elon the Hittite. Esau's pagan wives were a source of grief to Isaac and Rebekah.

Jacob deceives Isaac (27:1-28:5):

Isaac grew old and he could no longer see. One day he called Esau, his older son, to him, saying, "My son, I am now old, and I do not know when I might die. Therefore, take your bow and your quiver and go into the field and hunt venison and prepare for me the savory food that I love, and bring it to me that I may eat it and that I may give you your blessing before I die."

Rebekah, overhearing the conversation, called Jacob to her and said, "I heard your father tell Esau to bring venison and prepare savory food and he would give him his blessing. Therefore, my son, listen carefully, and do exactly what I tell you. Go to the flock and bring me two kids of the goats and I will make the savory food your father likes. Then you carry it in to him so that he may eat it and give you the blessing."

"But, Mother," Jacob replied, "my brother Esau is a hairy man, and I am a smooth man. What if my father touches me? I would appear to be deceiving him and he would curse me instead of blessing me." Rebekah said, "Any curse will be upon me. Only do what I have said quickly."

So Jacob brought the kids, and Rebekah prepared the food for Isaac. She took some of the clothes that belonged to Esau and put them on Jacob. She took the skins of the goats and put them on Jacob's hands and on the smooth part of his neck. Putting the food into his hands, she sent him in to his father.

Jacob said, "Father."

Isaac said, "Yes, who are you, my son?"

Jacob answered, "I am Esau your firstborn, and I have done as you told me. Now get up and eat of my venison so that you can bless me."

"How did you find a deer so quickly, my son?" Isaac asked.

"Because Jehovah your God gave me good speed."

"Come here, please," Isaac said, "so that I can feel you and see if you really are my son Esau." Jacob went close to his father, who felt him, and said, "The voice is that of Jacob, but the hands are the hands of Esau." Isaac could not tell it was Jacob because his hands felt hairy like Esau's hands.

"Are you my true son Esau?" Isaac asked.

"Yes, I am," Jacob replied.

"Bring me the food then that I may eat and drink, and then I will give you your blessing."

After he ate, Isaac said to Jacob, "Come near me and kiss me, my son."

When Jacob came over and kissed Isaac, his father said, "See, my son smells like the field which Jehovah has blessed. May God give you the dew of heaven and the fatness of the earth. Let nations serve you, and may you rule over your brethren. Cursed is everyone who curses you and let everyone be blessed who blesses you."

When Isaac finished blessing him, Jacob hurried out and was scarcely gone when in came Esau with a dish of savory meat for his father. He said, "Father, get up and eat the venison I have prepared, so that you can bless me."

Isaac, startled, said, "Who are you?"

Equally startled, Esau answered, "I am your son, your firstborn, Esau."

Isaac trembled violently and said, "Who then has already brought me venison which I have eaten? And I have blessed him, and it will be as I have said."

Esau cried aloud and said, "Please bless me also, my father."

"Your brother came and deceived me and took your blessing," Isaac replied.

Esau said, "Is he not truly named Jacob (Supplanter)? He has supplanted me these two times, taking first my birthright and now my blessing. Have you no blessing left for me?"

"What can I do for you? I have made him your ruler, and with grain and new wine I have endowed him. So what can I do for you, my son?"

Esau answered, "Haven't you one blessing for me, my father? Please bless me, too."

In answer, Isaac said, "You will dwell away from the richness of the earth and away from the dew of heaven. By your sword you will live, and you will serve your brother. Eventually, however, you will break loose and shake his yoke from your neck."

Esau hated Jacob for what he had done and he planned to kill Jacob as soon as Isaac died—which he expected to be fairly soon.

Rebekah, hearing about Esau's threats, called Jacob to her and said, "Your brother Esau is comforting himself, planning to kill you because of what you have done. Therefore, my son, do as I say, and go to my brother Laban, to Haran, and remain there a few days until your brother gets over his anger. Then I will send you word, and you can return."

Rebekah then went to Isaac and said, "I am worried to death because of the daughters of Heth (*Hittite women, referring to the wives of Esau*). If Jacob were to take a wife from among these pagan women, there would be no reason for me to live."

Isaac agreed, and calling Jacob to him, he said, "You will not take a wife from the daughters of Canaan. Get up and go to Paddan-aram, to the house of Bethuel, your mother's father, and take a wife from the daughters of Laban, your mother's brother. And may God bless you," Isaac continued, "and make you a multitude of people, and may He give you the blessings of Abraham so that you may inherit the land which God promised to Abraham." So Isaac sent Jacob away to Laban's house.

The blessing which Jacob got by deceit was neither the birthright itself nor the promises that had been given to Abraham and Isaac by God But the blessing was the one normally given from a father to the son who would inherit the property—therefore, closely tied to the birthright. Esau had sold his birthright, but obviously he was expecting and willing to accept the blessing from his father—and, almost certainly, the inheritance that normally went with it.

Rebekah had been told before the sons were born that the older would serve the younger (25:23); and Jacob had succeeded in acquiring the birthright and probably expected his father to give him this blessing to accompany it, but there is no excuse for the method that Rebekah and Jacob used to receive it. As we said earlier in the study of Genesis, the writer does not hide the sins of even the great heroes of faith. They, too, had frailties.

Since Isaac was trying to give the blessing (and, almost certainly, the inheritance) to Esau, it indicates he was planning to retire just as his own father had done when Isaac married Circumstances changed rapidly, however, with this event because the wrong son inherited the property in Isaac's eyes. Then Jacob is forced to flee for his life and Esau is left at home—but by the time Jacob returns, Esau has severed his direct ties with Isaac and is living in Mount Seir, while Jacob finds his father living at Mamre where Abraham had lived. So it seems that Isaac did not re-

tire at this point, and the property was kept for Jacob while he was away.

Though Jacob has just received the blessing and the inheritance, he leaves home as if he were a pauper. He himself later says that he left with only his staff in his hands (32:10). Remember the servant of ilbraham took ten camels loaded with precious things to go for a wife for Isaac, but now Jacob goes empty-handed because he is leaving in haste. His father told him to look for a wife, but his primary reason for leaving was to escape the wrath of Esau.

Chronology Note

Take time to calculate the age of Jacob and Esau at this time. They were not just young men ready to start a family. Enough data is given in the book of Genesis to determine their age and the age of Isaac.

- *Jacob and Esau were born when Isaac was sixty (25:26), and he lived to be 180 (35:28), and since this event took place when Isaac considered himself old, they had to be more than mere young men.*

- *Jacob was 130 years old when he went to Egypt in the days of Joseph (47:9).*

- *Joseph, at that time, was 39 (41:46; 41:29-30; 45:11).*

- *Joseph was, therefore, born when Jacob was 91.*

- *But Joseph was born at the close of the fourteen years that Jacob spent working for his wives in Paddan-aram (29:20, 30; 30:25; 31:41).*

- *Fourteen years subtracted from Jacob's age at Joseph's birth gives us the age 77 for Jacob and Esau at the time of this story.*

- *And since Isaac was sixty years older than they, he was 137 when he considered himself tld"and was ready to give his inheritance to his son.*

- *Esau thought his father was near death at this time, and he meant to wait until his death before avenging his wrath upon Jacob, but Isaac lived 43 more years!*

Esau marries a daughter of Ishmael (28:6-9):

Esau saw that Isaac blessed Jacob and sent him to Paddan-aram to get a wife. He also noted that Isaac had told Jacob *not* to take a *wife* of the daughters of Canaan and that Jacob had obeyed his father. Seeing that the daughters of Canaan were not pleasing to Isaac, Esau took, in addition to the wives he already had, Mahalath the daughter of Ishmael.

Jacob

(Genesis 28:10-36:43; 38:1-30; 48:1-49:33)

Though Isaac continues to live for several more years, the writer follows Jacob as he makes his way to Haran. Jacob and his family are the pre-dominant characters in chapters 28 through 36. Then the focus is turned upon Joseph, the favorite son of Jacob, until chapters 48 and 49 where we come back to Jacob to see his final acts and his death. Therefore we give the references where he is the main character in the heading for this section, but we will study our way through the rest of Genesis exactly as the events are told.

Jacob sees God at Bethel and makes a vow to Him (28:10-22):

Leaving Beersheba where his family lived, Jacob headed north along the ridge of the hill country. When he came to Luz he decided to spend the night because the sun was setting. He took one of the stones lying nearby and placed it under his head and went to sleep. During the night Jacob had a dream of divine origin: he saw a ladder reaching from earth to heaven with angels ascending and descending upon it. Jehovah stood at the head of the ladder, and He said to Jacob:

Promises repeated to Jacob:

Land
Nation
Spiritual

I am Jehovah, the God of your grandfather Abraham and of your father Isaac. The land where you are lying I will give to you and to your seed, and your seed will be as the dust of the earth. In you and in your seed all the families of the earth will be blessed. Also, I will be with you, I will keep you safe wherever you go, and I will bring you back into this land.

Jacob awoke with a start and was filled with fear. He said, "Without a doubt, Jehovah is in this place, and I did not know it. How awesome this place is! It is nothing less than the house of God, the very gate of heaven."

When Jacob arose early the next morning, he took the stone he had used for a pillow and set it upright and poured oil upon it. This act was designed to hallow the spot and to commemorate the vision of God which Jacob had seen. He called the name of the place Bethel *(house of God).* He made a vow, saying, "If God will be with me, and will look after me where I go, and will give me bread to eat and raiment to wear so that I can one day return to my father's house in peace, and if Jehovah will be my God, then this stone which I have set up for a pillar shall be God's house. And of all that God gives me, I will, without fail, give a tenth part back to Him."

By now God has made His three-fold promise to Abraham, to Isaac, and to Jacob. After Jacob, the nation of Israel (Jacob's descendants) becomes the recipient of the promises and their fulfillment. Promises about the particular seed, the one special descendant through whom all nations will be blessed, however, continues to be traced through the Bible, generation by generation, until the coming of the Christ.

Jacob meets Rachel (29:1-12):

Finally Jacob reached the vicinity of Haran. He saw a well where three flocks of sheep were waiting to be watered. The well was covered by a large rock. As he approached, Jacob asked the shepherds, "My brothers, where are you from?"

"We're from Haran," they replied.

"Do you know Laban, the grandson of Nahor?"

"Yes, we know him."

"How is he?" asked Jacob.

"He is well. As a matter of fact, that is Rachel his daughter coming now with the sheep."

Jacob urged the shepherds to go ahead and water their sheep, presumably because he wanted a chance to speak to Rachel without the shepherds being there. "Why don't you go ahead and water your sheep? The sun is still high; it is not time to bring the animals in. Go ahead and water them and go and feed them."

But the shepherds said, "No, we cannot water the sheep until all the flocks are gathered together, and they roll the stone back from the well. Then we will water our sheep."

By this time, Rachel *(her name means "ewe")* had arrived. When Jacob saw her and realized this was the daughter of Laban his mother's brother, he

went to the well, rolled the stone away, and watered the flock for Rachel. Then Jacob lifted up his voice and wept with joy and gratitude. He told Rachel that he was related to her father, that he was Rebekah's son. When she heard this, Rachel ran and told her father.

When Laban learned that Jacob had arrived, he ran to the well to meet him, embraced him, kissed him, and brought him to his home. Jacob told Laban all that had happened and why he was there. Laban's answer was: "Surely you are my bone and my flesh," in other words, "You are my relative, and you are, therefore, welcome in my home."

Map Assignment:

Go back to map #2 to see where Jacob has gone. He has traveled approximately 400 miles since he left Beersheba—and remember that he was walking—there is no mention of camels or other animals with him.

Possible site of ancient Bethel.

Jacob serves Laban for Rachel (29:13-20):

Laban welcomed Jacob into his house, but after a month, he said, "Just because you are my kinsman does not mean that you should be working for nothing. What salary would you like for me to pay you?"

There was one thing Jacob wanted more than money. Laban had two daughters, Leah, the older, and Rachel. Leah's eyes were such that they detracted from her appearance, but Rachel was beautiful. Jacob loved Rachel, so he said, "I will serve you seven years for your younger daughter Rachel."

Laban said, "It is better for me to give her to you than to a stranger. Stay with *me*" (or as we would say, "It's a deal."

So Jacob served Laban seven years for Rachel and considered it a bargain. The time seemed short because of his love for her.

Remember that Laban was one of the ones primarily involved in the arrangement for Rebekah to become Isaac's wife (24:50). At that time the servant had come with great wealth to prove that his master's son was a rich man and that Rebekah would do well to go with him. Now, years later, Jacob comes for a wife, but he comes alone, and with no riches to show. Jacob was even richer than his father had been at the same age, because Isaac had continued to prosper, and Jacob was to inherit his father's possessions—but Jacob had left home fleeing for his life. He did not take time to gather rich gifts lest Esau take the opportunity to kill him. A month goes by with Jacob working for Laban, but receiving no pay. Finally Laban inquired about his plans by offering to pay him a salary.

The next morning, surprise! It was Leah that Jacob had! He rushed to Laban and said, "What is the meaning of this? Did I not serve you for Rachel? Why then have you deceived me?"

Laban replied, "In our area, it is just not done to give the younger in marriage before the older. Fulfill the week for Leah and then I will give you Rachel also, with the understanding that you will serve me seven more years."

Jacob had very little choice if he wanted to have Rachel, so he fulfilled the week for Leah, and then Laban gave him Rachel also. Jacob took Rachel as his wife, and he loved her more than Leah, and he served Laban seven more years. Laban gave Rachel a maidservant also, named Bilhah.

Add the new names to your family tree:

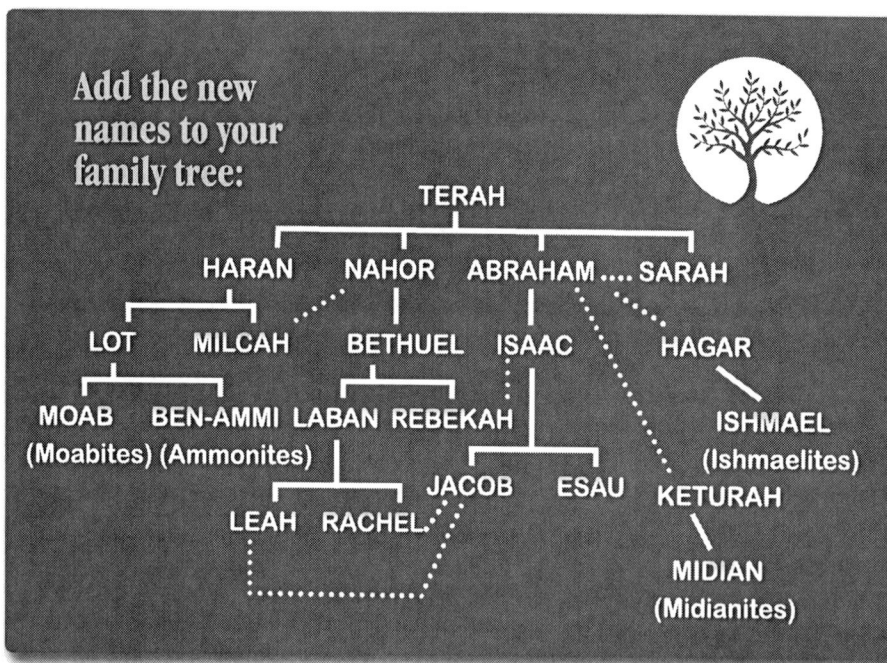

Jacob is deceived (29:21-30):

At the end of the seven years, Jacob went to Laban and said, "Give me my wife, for I have kept my agreement with you."

Laban gathered the men of the area and made a wedding feast for Jacob. Later that evening, Laban took Leah, his older daughter, and brought her to Jacob, and he went to bed with her. Laban also gave Leah a handmaid named Zilpah.

Many marvel that Jacob could be so easily deceived. The brief description of the wedding sounds similar to the general way in which marriages were often accomplished in that day. After a considerable period of feasting, the bride was brought to the nuptial tent where the groom waited. If this were the case with Jacob and Leah, it was dark; she would have been covered with a veil until she got into the tent. It is not at all unusual for sisters' voices to sound alike, particularly if a little effort is made to enhance the similarity. Leah had to be partners with her father in the effort to deceive, and her cooperation made it easy to deceive Jacob. Rachel is the one we wonder about. Where was she during this deception? Laban must have had her locked away!

Thus Jacob's deception of his own father was now visited upon him. Also the foundation was laid for a deep-seated enmity between the sisters, and a rivalry between them for the love of their husband. The names of Jacob's sons bear testimony to the enmity and strife that went on in his household between his wives. Their story is a sad one.

Leah bears children (29:31-35):

When Jehovah saw that Leah was loved little in comparison to Rachel, He opened her womb while Rachel remained barren. Soon Leah had a son which she named Reuben, meaning: "See, a son!" because she said, "Jehovah has looked upon my affliction. Now my husband will love me."

After a time she bore again and said, "Jehovah has heard *(shamah)* that I am hated and has therefore given me this son also." So she named him Simeon *(Hebrew: Shimeon)*.

She had a third son and named him Levi, because she said, "Now this time my husband will be joined *(lavah)* to me because I have given him three sons."

Again she conceived and had a son and said, "This time I will praise *(hodah)* Jehovah." So she named the child Judah *(Jehudah)*.

Conflicts continue between Leah and Rachel (30:1-24):

When Rachel saw that she had no children, she envied her sister, and said to Jacob, "Give me children, or else I am going to die."

Her statement made Jacob angry, so he said, "Who do you think I am, God?"

Rachel answered, "Look, here is my maid-servant Bilhah. Go to bed with her so that I can have children by her."

> **Leah's Children:**
>
> **Reuben**
> **Simeon**
> **Levi**
> **Judah**
> **Issachar**
> **Zebulun**
>
> **Dinah**

> **Sons of the handmaids:**
>
> **Bilhah:**
> **Dan**
> **Naphtali**
>
> **Zilpah:**
> **Gad**
> **Asher**

Jacob took Bilhah as a servant wife *(concubine)*, and she conceived and bore a son. Rachel said, "God has judged *(dan)* me and has made things right," so she called the child Dan.

Again Bilhah bore a son, and Rachel said, "With superhuman wrestlings I have wrestled *(niphtal)* with my sister, and I have won." Therefore she called him Naphtali.

When Leah saw that she had stopped bearing children for a while, she countered Rachel by giving Jacob her maidservant Zilpah. When Zilpah bore a son, Leah said, "How fortunate!" She named the baby Gad *(Fortune)*.

Soon Zilpah had another son, and Leah said, "How happy *(asher)* I am! Now all the ladies will call me happy." So she called him Asher.

About this time, Reuben, who was still quite small, went out in the field during the wheat harvest and found some mandrakes and brought them to his mother. When Rachel learned that Leah had mandrakes, she went to her and said, "Give me, please, some of your son's mandrakes."

Leah said, "Isn't it enough for you that you have taken away my husband? Will you also take away my son's mandrakes as well?"

Rachel said, "Very well. Jacob can sleep with you tonight in return for your son's mandrakes."

That evening, when Jacob came from the field, Leah met him and said, "You must come to me tonight because I have hired you with my son's mandrakes." Jacob went to bed with her that night, and, once again, Leah conceived and bore a son. She said, "God has given me my hire *(sachar)* because I gave my handmaid to my husband." So she called this son Issachar.

At the birth of her sixth son, Leah said, "God has given me a good dowry. Now my husband will dwell *(zabal)* with me, because I have borne him six sons," and she called him Zebulun.

Then Leah had a daughter also, and she named her Dinah.

God heard Rachel's plea and enabled her to conceive and have a son. She said, "God has taken away my reproach." She named the child Joseph, saying, "Jehovah add *(Joseph)* to me another son."

The mandrake plant is very common in Canaan. The fruit resembles little yellow apples about the size of a nutmeg. They were considered then, and now, by the Bedouins as an aid to child-bearing (K & D., Vol. p. 222).

Notice how close together these first eleven sons were in age. The next part of the story begins by saying, "when Rachel had borne Joseph..." Jacob considered himself ready to leave because he had fulfilled his obligation to work the extra seven years for Rachel. That means that all these sons were born during these seven years. It is clear, therefore, that the pregnancies of the four mothers overlapped. For example, Bilhah must have been expecting Dan before Judah was born, and then Zilpah was expecting Gad before Naphtali was born, and so forth.

Laban pays Jacob wages (30:25-43):

When Rachel had borne Joseph, Jacob went to Laban and said, "Let me go now, so that I may return to my own country. Give me my wives and my children for whom I have worked, because you know the quality of the work I have done for you."

Rachel's Children:

Joseph
Benjamin

(Benjamin was not born until they were back in the land of Canaan.)

Laban said, "If it is suitable to you, I would like for you to remain with me because I can tell that God has blessed me for your sake. Set what I should pay you, and I will give it to you."

Jacob answered, "You know how I have served you and how well your livestock has prospered since I came to be with you. You had just a little when I came, and now it has come to be a multitude. Jehovah has blessed me every way I have turned, but now I must be concerned about building up my own estate."

Laban replied, "What shall I give you?"

Jacob answered, "Do not *give* me anything! Instead, let me make a suggestion. If it is satisfactory with you, I will continue to look after your flocks. I will pass through the flocks today and I will remove every spotted and speckled animal from among the goats and every black one from among the sheep, and this will be my hire. I will put my integrity on the line: if you find any animal not of those colors among my livestock, then count it stolen."

Laban readily agreed, "Let it be as you have said." Laban went through his herds and flocks and separated all the animals that Jacob was due to receive for wages. Then he removed Jacob's animals three days' journey from his own, and Jacob fed the rest of Laban's flocks. Laban's own sons cared for Jacob's animals, at least at first.

Jacob decided to take his own measures to make his flocks increase. He took saplings of trees and peeled strips from the bark and then placed these striped rods at the watering troughs where the flocks came to drink. The animals conceived before the rods and brought forth multi-colored animals. Jacob also caused Laban's flocks to feed where they could look upon his own flocks of multi-colored animals. As soon as he had enough animals of the proper color for a flock, he put them apart from Laban's flocks. Another measure he took to strengthen his flock was to use the striped rods only when the stronger of the animals conceived. Gradually Jacob became very wealthy, possessing in addition to his flocks and herds, camels and donkeys, men-servants and maid-servants.

Most sheep were white, and most goats were black Comparatively few sheep were black and few goats were white or spotted Therefore, this was a wise suggestion on Jacob's part. He would get enough animals to start his flocks, but not enough to deplete Laban's stock too badly.

Laban wanted God's blessings to continue on his possessions, so he wanted Jacob's help with his animals, but he did not want the multi-colored stock to be close enough to breed with his own lest the number of multi-colored animals increase. Such behavior was entirely consistent with Laban's character and with his dealings with Jacob. (See 30:40; 31:7.)

Jacob's actions were based upon ideas held until very recent times: that when animals (or people) conceive, they are influenced by what they see at the time. Jacob thought that by their seeing the black and white stripes in the wood, the animals would produce spotted and speckled animals. There is no evidence that such efforts work It was God who caused Jacob to be blessed Choosing the stronger animals probably does not mean he examined each animal to choose the stronger, but that he used the rods in the spring. Young conceived in the spring and born in the fall tended to be stronger than those conceived in the fall and born in the spring, at the end of a long, cold winter.

Jacob flees from Laban (31:1-55):

As Jacob's flocks increased, he began hearing complaints Laban's sons were making: "Jacob has taken everything our father had. All this wealth he has came from our father's things." Jacob could also detect that Laban's own attitude toward him was changing.

About this time, Jehovah appeared to Jacob and said, "Return to the land of your fathers and to your relatives, and I will be with you." So Jacob called Leah and Rachel to come to him in the field where his flocks were, and he said:

I can tell your father does not like me as he did, but the God of my father has been with me. You know how diligently I have served your father. He has deceived me and changed my wages ten times, but God did not let him hurt me. If he said the spotted animals would be my wages, then that was the color the animals produced.

At the time the flocks conceived, I had a dream in which the he-goats that mate with the flock were speckled, spotted, and grizzled. And the angel of the Lord said to me, "Jacob, look and see: all the he-goats which mate with the flock are striped, speckled, and mottled, because I have seen all Laban is doing to you. I am the God of Bethel where you poured oil upon a pillar of rock, where you made a vow to me. Now get up and leave this land and return to the land where you were born."

Rachel and Leah responded: "Is there still some inheritance left for us in our father's house? Does he not regard us as complete strangers? He sold us and has gotten his full value from the price you paid for us. All the riches which God has taken from our father now belongs to us and to our children. Whatever God has told you to do, do it."

Jacob's sons by age:

Reuben
Simeon
Levi
Judah
Dan
Naphtali
Gad
Asher
Issachar
Zebulun
Joseph
Benjamin

Jacob needed no further encouragement. Setting his children and his wives upon camels, he led away all the livestock he had accumulated. With all his possessions, he headed back home to Isaac his father in the land of Canaan, deliberately picking a time to leave when Laban was three days' journey away, shearing sheep, lest he be stopped. As she was leaving, Rachel stole the idols that belonged to her father, and the whole encampment of Jacob sneaked away from Laban and headed for Mount Gilead on the eastern side of the Jordan River. *(Look on your map to see Haran and the mountains of Gilead.)*

On the third day, Laban returned home and learned that Jacob had fled. Taking his relatives with him, Laban set out to pursue Jacob. Seven days later he overtook him in the mountains of Gilead. The night before Laban caught up with Jacob, God spoke to him in a dream and said, "See that you do not speak forcefully to Jacob to change his plans."

When Laban entered Jacob's camp, he said, "Why did you sneak away and take my daughters as if they were captives you had taken with the sword? Why didn't you tell me you were leaving, so that I could have sent you away with merriment and songs? You did not even let me kiss my children goodbye. I could do harm to you, but the God of your father spoke to me last night and told me not to harm you or to seek to change your mind.

"But," continued Laban, "there is another matter: though you wanted very much to return to your father's house, why did you steal my gods?"

Jacob answered, "I left secretly to keep you from taking your daughters from me by force. As for your gods, if you find them with anyone, that person will

be put to death. Before our relatives, bring out what you claim is yours and take it." But Jacob did not know that Rachel had stolen the idols.

Laban went into Jacob's tent, and into Leah's tent, and into the tents of Bilhah and Zilpah, but he did not find the idols. Then he entered Rachel's tent. She had put the idols in the camel's saddle, and she was sitting upon them. Laban searched all around the tent, but he did not find the idols. Rachel said, "Sir, please do not be angry with me for not getting up, but the manner of women is upon me." So Laban did not find the idols.

Mountains of Gilead.

Jacob was very angry with Laban, not only for making what appeared to be a false accusation, but for pursuing him, and for all the injustices of the past. He said, "What great wrong have I done to you to make you chase after me so hotly? Now that you have rummaged through all my things, what have you found? Set it out here so that all of us can see it! During these twenty years that I have been with you, I have taken good care of your livestock. Any loss you had, I bore it. During the day the drought wore me out, and by night the frost was upon me, and I never got enough sleep. Twenty years I have been in your house. I served fourteen years for your two daughters and six years for your flocks. You have changed my wages over and over again. If the God of my fathers had not been with me, you would have sent me away empty. God has seen my problems with you, and He rebuked you last night."

Laban did not answer Jacob's bitter charges. He said, "These are my daughters; these children are my flesh and blood; the flocks are my flocks, and all that you see is mine. How could I do anything to these daughters of mine or to their children? Come and let us make an agreement of peace, you and I, and let it be a matter of record between us."

Jacob agreed, and he took a stone and made it a pillar. Then he said to his brethren, "Pile up stones." They made a pile of rocks and ate together by the pile. Laban called the pile of rocks "Jegarsahadutha" ("Heap of Testimony" in Aramaic, Laban's native language). Jacob called it "Galeed" ('Heap of Testimony" in Hebrew). The place was also called "Mizpah" (the Watch Tower) because Laban said, "May Jehovah watch between me and you while we are absent one from another. If you mistreat my daughters, or if you marry other wives, then our agreement is canceled. See, God is witness between us."

Laban continued: "Let this pile be witness that I will not pass this pile and this pillar to harm you, and you will not pass it to harm me. May the God of Abraham, and of Nahor, the God of their father, judge between us." Jacob swore by the God whom Isaac feared.

Jacob offered a sacrifice and called his brethren to eat bread. They ate together and spent the night in the mountains. Early the next morning, Laban kissed his grandchildren and his daughters goodbye and left to return to his home.

There are several interesting things to note in this story:

- *Jacob traveled very rapidly here as he began his journey (he had covered between 300 and 400 miles before Laban caught up with him in the mountains of Gilead).Laban left three days later and caught him in seven days, but Laban was traveling with all adults and no flocks and herds. Jacob was hurrying to get away from Laban, but we will see him slow down in his journey very soon.*

- *Though Leah and the others were from the same background as Rachel, it was Rachel who stole her father's gods. The story is certainly not flattering to her. What she told her father was that she was having her monthly period and could not get up. Laban accepted that explanation because women were considered unclean at such a time.*

- *It was an extraordinary insult for Laban to accept Jacob's offer to let him search the tents—and then actually to rummage around through his possessions! No wonder Jacob was angry.*

It is a little difficult to know whether Laban was referring to Jehovah God here as part of his oath. Note some details:

- *From this passage it sounds as if the God of Abraham, the God of Nahor, and the God of their father Terah were the same.*

- *It may be significant, however, that Jacob chose to swear by the God of his father Isaac.*

- *Notice that these stolen idols obviously belonged to Laban, and it is a logical assumption that he was in the habit of worshiping them.*

- *There is also a passage in Joshua 24:14-15 that makes us wonder what kind of religious background the family had before they left Ur of the Chaldees. In that passage, Joshua warns the people to put away the gods their fathers served "on the other side of the flood," almost certainly referring to their fathers on the other side of the Euphrates.*

- *Yet, Abraham and Isaac thought it would be far better for their sons to marry wives from among their relatives in Paddan-aram than for them to marry the idolatrous women of the land of Canaan.*

- *So, even though there were idolatrous concepts mixed into their religion, there must still have been a strong awareness of Jehovah in the thinking of Abraham's relatives.*

The covenant described here illustrates again the way covenants were usually made in that day. Notice how the parties involved in the covenant stated the terms, swore to those terms, and then ate together as a sign the covenant had been sealed. So far as the record goes, this is the last contact between the descendants of Nahor and the descendants of Abraham.

Chronology Note

Determine how long Jacob was gone from Canaan, and how the years were spent:

- *He worked a total of _____ years for Rachel (29:18, 27).*

- *The total number of years he worked for Laban was _____ years (31:38); so after his years of working for his wives, he worked _____ years for his animals.*

- *Do you remember that when he fled from Esau, Rebekah suggested that he go and stay "a few days" until Esau's anger turned away (27:44)?*

Esau is coming! (32:1-21):

As Jacob went on his way, the angels of God met him. When he saw them, he said, "This is God's host *(company, multitude)*." So he called the place Mahanaim *(two hosts, or companies),* because God's company of angels had joined Jacob's company of people.

Now as Jacob was returning home, his thoughts turned to the trouble and strife he had with Esau before he left home. As a way of seeking peace, he sent messengers to Esau, who was now living in Mount Seir, telling them to give Esau this message: "I have stayed with Laban until now. I have many possessions, and I have sent to tell you, my lord Esau, so that I may find favor with you."

The messengers returned with an ominous report: "We came to your brother Esau, and he is coming to meet you, and he has 400 men with him."

Jacob was terrified! The last time he saw his brother, Esau was planning to kill him. Now he was coming with 400 men! He must be planning trouble! Jacob immediately divided his people and possessions into two groups. His thought was, "If Esau smites one company, then the one which is left may escape."

Jacob did not rely merely upon his own wisdom and upon measures which he could personally take; he also called upon Jehovah:

O God of my grandfather Abraham and of my father Isaac, O Jehovah, who told me, "Return to your country and to your people, and I will do you good." I am not worthy of the least of your favors, and of all the truth you have shown me, because I passed over this Jordan with only my staff, and now I have grown to two companies. Deliver me, I beg you, from the hand of my brother Esau. I am afraid that he will come and smite my people, the mother with the children. You told me you would do me good, and would make my seed as the sand of the sea.

That night Jacob prepared a series of gifts for Esau. He prepared several droves of animals: two hundred she-goats and twenty he-goats; two hundred ewes and twenty rams; thirty milk camels and their colts; forty cows and ten bulls; twenty female donkeys and ten foals. He placed servants over each group of animals, separated them, and sent them one group at a time. He told the servants to present each drove separately, and with each drove, the servants were told: "When Esau my brother asks, 'To whom do you belong? Where are you going? Whose are these animals?' Then you are to answer, "They belong to your servant Jacob. They are a present for my lord Esau, and your servant Jacob is coming behind us."

Jacob hoped to appease Esau by these offerings. The presents he had prepared passed on ahead, and he remained in camp, that is, he did not travel further until he knew what would happen next.

Notice how many place names are begun in the book of Genesis. This is one more reason for calling the book "Genesis"—the Book of Beginnings. We have watched as the name Beersheba became established for the village that grew up around the wells Abraham and Isaac dug. Then we saw Bethel named by Jacob when he saw the dream of a ladder reaching to heaven. Then as Laban and Jacob made their covenant, Jacob named the area on the eastern side of the Jordan, Galeed. From this time forward, the term Gilead will be used for all or portions of the territory on the east side of the Jordan. Now we find Jacob naming Mahanaim. Continue watching as he names more places. Since Jacob's descendants inherited the land, the names given by the patriarchs were retained through the years even if others may have called the places by other names in the intervening years.

Mahanaim is one of the places that has never been definitely located by archaeologists, so there is no way to be sure where it would fit on the map. Some maps show it south of the Jabbok River, but the story shows that some time passed between this appearance of God to Jacob and his crossing of the Jabbok (32:22-23). Therefore, Mahanaim was located somewhere north of the Jabbok River, in the highlands of Gilead.

The territory of Mount Seir was the possession of Esau, who was now called Edom. From this time on, until very late in Old Testament history, we will find Edomites living in the mountainous region south of the Dead Sea.

Map Assignment:

- Label the plateau on the east side of the Jordan Gilead.
- Label the Jabbok River.
- Mark Mahanaim a little north of the Jabbok and in Gilead.
- Label Mount Seir and the territory of Edom.

Jacob wrestles with an angel (32:22-32):

Later that same night, Jacob arose and took his wives and concubines and their children and crossed the ford of the Jabbok River. After sending his family over the stream, plus all his possessions, he remained alone on the north side of the river.

During the night a "man" came and wrestled with Jacob until daybreak. When the man saw that he did not overcome Jacob, he touched Jacob's hip joint and threw the hip out of socket. The man said, "Let me go, for the dawn is breaking."

Jacob, obviously aware that this "man" was more than he appeared, said, "I will not let you go unless you bless me."

The man said, "What is your name?"

"Jacob."

"Your name will no longer be Jacob (Supplanter), but Israel (he who strives with God) because you have striven with God and with men and have overcome."

Jacob said, "Tell me your name."

The man answered, "Why do you ask me about my name?" And he blessed him there.

Jacob called the place Peniel (Peni=face of + El=God), because he said, "I have seen God face to face, and I am still alive."

The sun arose as he passed over Penuel (alternate spelling for Peniel), and he limped on the leg that had been touched. Therefore, Israel's descendants do not eat the sciatic nerve of their animals because the "man" touched the hollow of Jacob's thigh in the sinew (nerve) of his hip.

Jacob's wrestling with the angel was parallel to the fervent prayer that Jacob was offering to God that he be spared from the hand of Esau. The angel who *came to wrestle with him and Jacob's "overcoming" were physical demonstrations of what he was accomplishing through his prayer. This was God's message when He changed Jacob's name to Israel with the explanation: "You have striven with God and have overcome." God was saying, "Jacob, you have striven with me in prayer—and I have heard you. You have overcome. You need not be afraid." But Jacob was too afraid at the moment to realize what God was saying.*

We see a lesson here that is taught often throughout the word of God: Our physical enemies are not the ones whom we should fear. God is the One with whom we must contend (strive), and if we succeed with God, then we will overcome the world, not by physical means, but, as Jacob learned, by relying upon God

Now that Jacob's name has been changed, the two names will be used interchangeably for the man himself and his descendants will be called Israelites "instead of "Jacobites."

Jacob and Esau are reconciled (33:1-17):

The dreaded meeting came to pass. Word came, "Esau is coming" *(will arrive very quickly now).* Jacob grouped the children with their mothers: first, the two handmaids with their children, then Leah with hers, and, last of all, Rachel and Joseph. *(Name the sons and their mothers and see if you could have placed them in the correct order.)* Jacob went before them and bowed himself seven times until he came to Esau. Imagine his joy and relief when Esau ran to him, hugged him, and kissed him, and wept. Esau looked up at Jacob's family and said, "Who are these people with you?"

"These are the children God has graciously given to your servant," he replied. Then Jacob had each wife draw near with her children. When Esau had met all Jacob's wives and children, he said, "What did you mean by all those people I met?"

"I hoped to find favor with my Lord Esau."

"I have enough, my brother. You keep your things."

Jacob answered, "No, I beg you, if you are not angry with me, then please receive my present, because I have seen your face as the face of God, and you were pleased with me. Please accept my gift because God has dealt graciously with me, and I have more than enough." Finally Esau agreed to take the gift.

Esau said, "Let us be on our way, and I will lead the way before you."

Jacob replied, "My lord, the children are young, and the flocks and herds have their young. If I overdrive them, the flocks will die. Let my lord please go on before me, and I will proceed at a leisurely pace as the herds and flocks will permit, until I come to Mount Seir."

Esau answered, "Well, then let me leave some of the people who are with me."

But Jacob said, "There is no need for that."

So Esau returned toward Mount Seir, and Jacob journeyed on to Succoth *(booths, huts)* and built him a house, and made booths *(perhaps corrals, or shelters)* for his cattle. Therefore the place was called Succoth.

In our English language, the two terms the brothers used to describe their possessions are alike: "enough." But in the original, Esau said, "I have enough," meaning "all I need, plenty." Jacob used a stronger expression as he said, "I have everything—all!" To see Esau as a beloved brother welcoming him home made Jacob feel that he had no need for anything else in life. Every need was filled.

Jacob comes to Shechem and buys land (33:18-20):

Finally Jacob came to Shechem and encamped before the city. He bought the tract of land where he was camped from the children of Hamor, Shechem's father, for a hundred pieces of money. He spread his tent there, built an altar, and called it El Elohe-Israel *(that is, "God, the God of Israel")*. Remember that Shechem was where God first promised the land of Canaan to Abraham (12:7).

This is the second time one of the patriarchs has bought a tract of land; the first was when Abraham bought the field containing the Cave of Machpelah which they were using as a family burial place. Remember this tract of land. The day will come when Joseph's bones will be buried here (Josh. 24:32).

Notice that this time Jacob refers to God as the "God of Israel" rather than the "God of Abraham and of Isaac." Through the experiences he has had, God has become very personal to Jacob.

Simeon and Levi smite the men of Shechem (34:1-31):

Dinah, Jacob's daughter, went out to see the daughters of the land. While she was there, Shechem, the son of Hamor, saw her and seduced her. Shechem loved Dinah and comforted her after his actions. He spoke to his father saying, "Get me this girl for a wife."

Jacob heard that Shechem had defiled Dinah, but his sons were in the field with the cattle, so he did nothing until they came in. Jacob's sons were very angry when they heard what Shechem had done.

Modern city of Nablus, site of ancient Shechem.

Hamor, at the request of his son Shechem, came out to negotiate with Jacob for Dinah's hand in marriage. He said, "My son's heart yearns for your daughter. Please give her to him for a wife, and make marriages with us. You may dwell in our land anywhere you choose, and conduct your business."

Shechem said to Jacob and to Dinah's brothers, "Let me find favor with you. I will pay you whatever dowry you ask, but give me the girl for a wife."

Jacob's sons spoke deceitfully, however, saying, "We cannot allow our sister to marry one who is uncircumcised. That would not be appropriate for us. Only on one condition will we agree to do what you ask: If every male among you will be circum-cised, then we will give our daughters to you and take your daughters for us and dwell in the land and be a part of you. If you won't agree, then we will take Dinah, and we will be gone."

These words pleased Hamor and Shechem. The young man did not waste any time because he had such fondness for Jacob's daughter. Shechem had great influence in his father's house, so he and Hamor talked with the men of their city at the gate and said, "These men are at peace with us. If we meet their condition, that each one of us be circumcised, then will not their cattle and their possessions be ours?"

All the men agreed to their proposal, and every man was circumcised. On the third day, when the men of Shechem were sore, Simeon and Levi took their swords and attacked the city by surprise and killed all the men. They slew Hamor and Shechem and took Dinah from Shechem's house. The sons of Jacob came and looted the city because Shechem had defiled Dinah. They took their flocks and herds, all their wealth, and their wives and children.

Jacob was very upset with his sons, and he said to Simeon and Levi: "You have made me to stink to the people who live in this land. Here we live among the Canaanites and the Perizzites, few in number, and now they will rise up against me and kill me."

His sons replied, "Should he treat our sister as if she were a harlot?" In their minds, this was the only justification needed for their actions.

The people of Canaan would have been very glad to become one people with this wealthy tribe. The men of Shechem wanted to intermarry with Jacob's family—let us take your daughters as our wives and you take our daughters for your sons. " The Philistines had wanted treaties of peace with first Abraham and then Isaac. But this was not God's plan for these people. He had deliberately separated Abraham from his relatives so that his descendants could develop as a distinct nation. If they had intermarried regularly with the Canaanites, they would soon have been absorbed into one or another of the Canaanite tribes. Remember this about the Canaanites, because the circumstances will be different when the family moves to Egypt.

Chronology Note

This episode with Dinah and Shechem helps us establish a time frame of this period:

- *Joseph was approximately six years old when Jacob left Haran (30:22-25; 31:41) and he was seventeen when he was sold as a slave (37:2).*

- *That means there were eleven years spent at Succoth, Shechem, Bethel, and then at Hebron (33:17, 1820; 35:6, 27) before Joseph was sold. Jacob built a house at Succoth, and he bought land at Shechem, but we do not know how long he lived at either place, nor how long he lived at Shechem before the defilement of Dinah.*

- *Most of those eleven years must have been spent at Succoth and Shechem, before the family journeyed on to Hebron, because it is apparent that at least some of Jacob's sons were grown young men by now. They would not have been grown for a few years after returning to Canaan since even Reuben, the oldest, would have been only about twelve years old at the time of Jacob's meeting with Esau.*

Jacob goes to Bethel (35:1-15):

God commanded Jacob to rise up and go to Bethel, adding, "Make an altar there unto God who appeared to you when you fled from Esau your brother."

Therefore Jacob said to his household, "Put away all the foreign gods which are among you and purify yourselves, and change your garments. We are going to Bethel. There I will build an altar unto God who came to my rescue when I was in great trouble."

The people of Jacob's encampment gathered their idols and the amulets they wore as ear rings, and Jacob buried them under an oak which was near Shechem. The family traveled southward to Bethel, and, because the terror of God was upon the cities, no one pursued them to take vengeance for their cruelty to the men of Shechem.

So Jacob came to Luz where he built an altar. He called the place El-bethel *(the God of Bethel)* because it was there God was revealed to him when he fled from Esau. While they were at Bethel, Deborah, Rebekah's nurse, died and was buried under an oak. The name of the place was called Allon-bacuth *(the oak of weeping).*

God appeared to Jacob again and confirmed that his new name would be Israel. He said, "I am God

Promise repeated here:

Nation

Land

Almighty: be fruitful and multiply. A company of nations will come from you, and kings will be among your descendants, and the land which I gave to Abraham and Isaac, I will give to your seed after you."

Jacob set up a stone pillar to commemorate the event and poured out a drink offering upon it. This appearance of God was at Bethel.

Death of Rachel (35:16-20):

As the family traveled on southward, Rachel went into labor. She began to have great difficulty delivering. Finally a baby boy was born. The midwife told her, "Don't be afraid; you have another son," but Rachel was dying. As she died, she named her son Benoni *(Son of my sorrow).* Jacob, however, called him Benjamin *(Son of my right hand).* Rachel was buried at Ephrath *(which is Bethlehem),* and Jacob set up a pillar to mark her grave.

Many years later, Jeremiah the prophet wrote: 'A voice is heard in Ramah, lamentation, and bitter weeping, Rach-

el weeping for her children; she refuses to be comforted for her children, because they are not" (Jer. 31:15). The following verses refer to Ephraim who was a grandson of Rachel through Joseph. By Jeremiah's day, Ephraim (the tribe) had been in captivity about one hundred years. Benjamin may also have been included in the prophet's words, because Ramah was likely the Ramah of Benjamin, and Benjamin was also Rachel's son. In Jeremiah's time Benjamin was sharing the bitter fate of Judah—the judgment of impending captivity. Jeremiah pictures Rachel weeping for the loss of her children to depict the very sad condition of the land.

In the days of Jesus, when Herod commanded the slaughter of the babes of Bethlehem, Matthew applies Jeremiah's statement about Rachel's weeping to that event as well, this time because it occurred in Bethlehem where Rachel was buried (Matt. 2:17-18).

Chronology Note

See the note after the story of Shechem and Dinah, and continue the thought:

- *The birth of Benjamin occurred during the interim between Jacob's leaving Labam's house and the time when Joseph was sold by his brothers. We* mention these two events because we can date the event by the ages of the sons.

- *Joseph was born right at the end of the second seven years that Jacob worked for his wives (30:22-25). That means he would have been about six years old when they left Laban to head back to Canaan and Reuben would have been about 12 years old (31:41).*

- *In these intervening years, Jacob lived at Succoth for a time and then at Shechem. While they were at Shechem, Dinah was old enough to be molested by the young man Shechem, and her brothers took their revenge (chapter 34).*

- *Since that event the family has spent some time at Bethel and are on their way to Hebron.*

- *Some time after they arrive in Hebron, Joseph is sold by his brethren—when he was 17 years old (37:2).*

- *That means Benjamin was still a very young child when Joseph was sold.*

Reuben's sin and Isaac's death (35:22-29):

Jacob remained in the vicinity of Ephrath for a time, beyond the tower of Eder. While they were there, Reuben committed adultery with Bilhah, and Israel heard of it.

Finally Jacob continued his journey and came to his father Isaac in Mamre. After living 180 years, Isaac died, and Esau and Jacob buried *him. (The place of his burial is not told here, but in Genesis 49:31, Isaac is included in the list of those buried at Hebron in the cave of Machpelah)*

Map Assignment:

Continue watching your map and labeling the places that have not yet been labeled:

- Penuel, where Jacob wrestled with an angel.
- Succoth, where Jacob built booths for his cattle.
- Shechem, where Jacob bought land and Dinah was molested.
- Bethel, where God appeared to Jacob again.
- Ephrath (later called Bethlehem), where Rachel died as Benjamin was born.
- Mamre (also known as Kiriath-arba and Hebron), where Jacob joins his father Isaac who is still living.

Once again, Jacob's sons are named: first, Leah's six sons, then Rachel's two sons, followed by Bilhah's two sons and last by Zilpah's two sons. *(Can you name them this way?)*

Bilhah may have been no more than fifteen or so years older than Reuben, who himself was no older than twenty-four years of age. Nothing is said at this point about anything Jacob did about the matter, but in Genesis 49 we learn that it was this sin which kept Jacob from giving the birthright to Reuben, though he was the firstborn son (49:4; see also 1 Chron. 5:1). As our story continues, watch to see which son receives that special blessing.

Chronology Note

- *When Isaac told Esau to go kill a deer and return to receive the blessing, it was because Isaac was "old" and ready to die.*

- *The whole family thought his death was near because Esau planned to wait until his father was dead to vent his wrath on Jacob, even though he was so angry (27:1-2, 41)—but Isaac lived more than forty years after that incident.*

Again, the writer of Genesis tells an event before it happened to keep from interrupting the main narrative.

- *Jacob was born when Isaac was 60 years old (25:26).*

- *Therefore, how old was Jacob when Isaac died (35:28)?*

- *But Jacob was only _____ years old when he went to Egypt and finally saw Joseph alive (47:9).*

- *Therefore, Isaac lived to see Joseph gone, but died thinking Joseph was dead because they had not yet learned he was alive in Egypt.*

The generations of Edom (36:1-43):

Only a few points need to be made from this chapter:

- The inspired writer continues to clings tenaciously to his story line. When characters come along who do not relate to the scheme of redemption, he shows us a little of their history and then returns to the main narrative.

- The wives of Esau are enumerated. They were "of the daughters of Canaan." Specifically, one was a Hittite, one was a Hivite, and one was a daughter of Ishmael (36:2-3).

- Five sons were born to Esau in the land of Canaan; then he moved southeast of Canaan to Mount Seir. Esau and Edom are two names for the same man. From this time on, the Edomites live in this section of the land south and southeast of the Dead Sea.

- One of Esau's descendants is named Amalek. There is no evidence, however, that this Amalek was the father of the Amalekites who play a role in Bible history on more than one occasion (see Exod. 17:8-16; 1 Sam. 15). Indeed, since Amalekites were among those smitten by the kings of Mesopotamia in the days of Abraham (Gen.14:7), they existed long before this Amalek was born.

- Seir was the name of one of the Horites, the original inhabitants of Edom. They were giants who were subsequently destroyed by the Edomites (Deut. 2:10-12).

- Kings of Edom are named. These kings ruled in Edom long before there was a king in Israel.

Judah and Tamar (38:1-30):

Chronology Note

Let us take this story out of the order in which it is recorded in the Bible text to avoid interrupting the story of Joseph. It is a story about a son of Jacob, just as the story of Simeon and Levi, the story of Reuben, and the story of Joseph are about his sons. This story is much shorter than the story of Joseph and it will fit well into the narrative here. The event, however, does not actually take place until

---

long after Joseph was sold, because Judah was not nearly old enough to have grown sons before that time. Let us take a moment to prove that point:

- *During the seven years in which Jacob's sons were born (29:27, 30; 30:25, 26), Judah was born fourth in line.*

- *The earliest he could have been born in those seven years was the fourth year, because he was Leah's fourth son.*

- *Joseph was born in the seventh year at the close of the period.*

- *Judah was therefore no more than three years older than Joseph.*

- *Since Joseph was seventeen when he was sold (37:2), Judah would have been about twenty.*

- *It was twenty-two years later when Judah saw Joseph again (42:3). (We will take time to follow the chronology of Joseph's time in Egypt as we study his story)*

- *It must have been near the end of the time while Joseph was in Egypt that this story occurs, because Judah's sons are grown and old enough to have a wife.*

It is interesting to think how these facts might relate to Judah's sympathy and understanding for Jacob's sadness when the safety and freedom of Benjamin is threatened.

At some time, Judah separated from his brothers and pitched his tent near an Adullamite whose name was Hirah. There he met a Canaanite named Shua, and Judah married his daughter. She conceived and had a son named Er; then one named Onan; and then a third son named Shelah while they lived at Chezib (or Achzib, located in the southern part of the Shephelah - Josh. 15:44).

When it was time for Er to marry, Judah arranged for him to have a woman named Tamar. But Er was wicked, and Jehovah slew him. Judah told his next son in line, Onan, to go to bed with Tamar and do the duty of a husband's brother and raise up a descendant to carry on the brother's name.

Onan realized that the child born through his union with Tamar would not bear his name, so when he went to bed with Tamar, he spilled the seed on the ground so that she would not conceive. He did not want to give a descendant to his brother. What Onan did was a very wicked thing in Jehovah's eyes, so God slew him also.

Judah told Tamar, "Remain a widow until Shelah my son is grown up." Judah did not want Tamar to have Shelah because he said to himself: "I don't want him to die like his brothers."

When Shelah was old enough to marry, and Tamar saw that Judah was not giving him to her as he had promised, she was moved to take desperate action. At about this same time, Judah's wife, the daughter of Shua, died. After a time of mourning, Judah went to Timnah where his men were shearing sheep, and his friend Hirah the Adullamite went with him.

Someone told Tamar, "Look, your father-in-law is going to Timnah to shear his sheep." She put off the garments of her widowhood, covered herself with a veil, and went to sit in the gate of Enaim which was on the way to Timnah.

When Judah saw her he thought she was a harlot because she was concealing her face. He went over to her and said, "Let me go to bed with you," not realizing he was talking to his daughter-in-law.

She said, "What will you give me to come in unto me?"

"I will give you a kid from the goats."

"Will you give me some guarantee that you will pay?" she asked.

"What guarantee shall I give you?"

Tamar replied, "Give me your signet ring, your cord, and your staff that you are holding."

Judah gave the items to her, lay with her, and then went on his way, but Tamar conceived by him. She put back on the clothes which marked her as a widow and went back to her father's house to await developments.

When Judah sent the goat in payment by the hand of his friend the Adullamite, there was no harlot to be found. Hirah asked the men of the area, "Where is the prostitute who was by the road at Enaim?"

The men answered, "There is no prostitute (kadeshah) around here."

When Judah heard, he said, "Well, that's her problem. I tried to pay her what I owed."

About three months later someone informed Judah: "Your daughter-in-law has behaved like a harlot, and she is pregnant through her fornication."

Judah was going to have no half-way measures in dealing with this outrage. "Bring her out to be burned," he said.

But when she was brought out, she sent word to her father-in-law, "The father of my child is the man to whom these items belong. See if you can identify the owner of this signet ring, its cord, and this staff."

When Judah saw them, he acknowledged that they were his and he said, "She is more righteous than I, because I did not give her Shelah my son." Judah did not go in unto Tamar again, though, presumably, she lived under his protection as his wife after this.

When she went into labor to deliver the baby, there were twins in her womb. One of the twins put forth a hand, and the midwife, thinking that he was about to be born, tied a scarlet thread around his wrist so they would not confuse the babies after they were born. To her surprise, he drew his arm back in, and the other baby was born first. She said, "So you made a breach for yourself, did you?" Therefore his name was Perez (*to make a*

breach), and his brother's name was Zerah.

The practice of a man taking his brother's widow and raising up seed to inherit the brother's estate dates back to very ancient times. The law of Moses was not yet in effect, but the custom was already wide spread. In the law we find God's regulations regarding it (Deut. 25:5-10), and allusions are made to it in later Scriptures (Ruth, chapters 3 and 4; Matt. 22:23-33, e.g.). The purpose of the custom and the law was to provide an heir when a man died leaving no heir. As Moses put it, the name of the dead man would "'not be blotted out" (Deut. 25:6). The first child would bear the name of the dead man; the rest of the children would bear the name of the second man. Though here and in Deuteronomy 25 the term "brother" is used, in Ruth, the expression "nearest kin" is used. Onan was willing to have sexual relations with Tamar, but not in order to provide a descendant for his dead brother. Thus he perverted God's purpose in this arrangement, and God slew him for it.

The word used for prostitute in verse 21 is a different word from harlot in verse 15. The second word signifies a woman who engaged in fornication with men as an act of worship—a kadeshah—whereas a

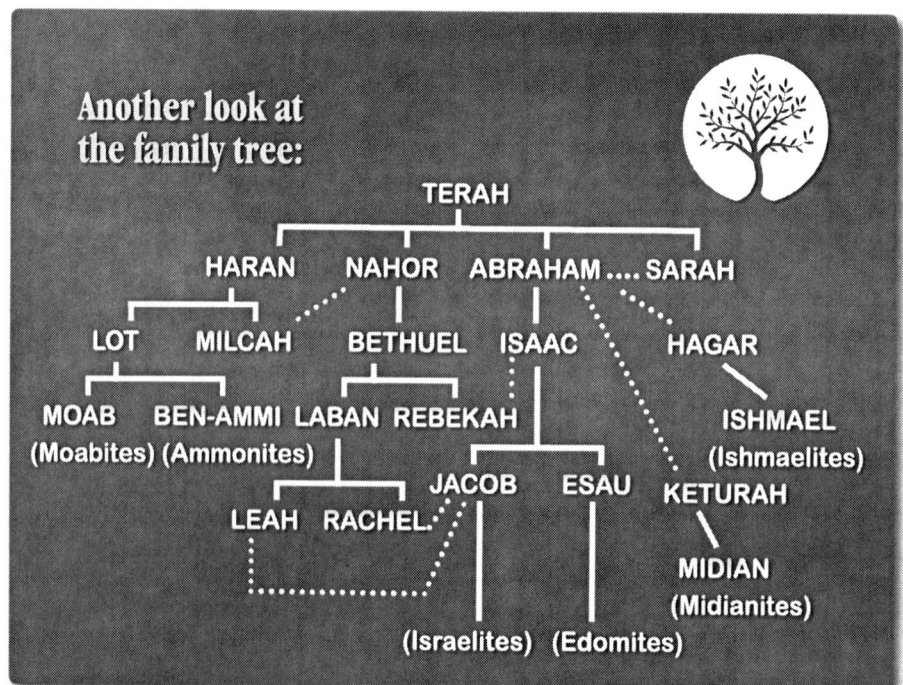

Another look at the family tree:

TERAH

HARAN   NAHOR   ABRAHAM .... SARAH

LOT   MILCAH   BETHUEL   ISAAC   HAGAR

MOAB   BEN-AMMI   LABAN   REBEKAH   ISHMAEL
(Moabites) (Ammonites)   (Ishmaelites)

JACOB   ESAU   KETURAH

LEAH   RACHEL   MIDIAN
(Midianites)

(Israelites) (Edomites)

harlot is one who merely sells her services—a zonah. It seems that Tamar dressed herself as a harlot, but when Judah's friend took the payment for her services, he asked for a kadeshah—one who performed ritual fornication. Rahab in the days of Joshua was a harlot (a zonah), not a kadeshah (Josh. 2:1).

The lineage of the Christ comes through Perez (see Matt. 1:3).

Joseph
(Gen. 37:1-36; 39:1-50:26)

Though the remaining story in Genesis is about Joseph, the writer of Genesis calls it "the generations of Jacob" (37:2). As in the other places where similar expressions are found, the meaning is not, "Here is the story of Jacob's beginnings," but rather, "Here are further developments in the life of Jacob." The writer thus indicates that Jacob is the patriarch whose history is told in the remainder of the book, but that history is focused on his son Joseph. The word "patriarch" means "father-ruler." We have made the story of Joseph a separate heading in the period of the patriarchs because so much of the book of Genesis is devoted to his life, but he is not listed as one of the "father-rulers" of the Israelites. The "fathers" of the Israelites were Abraham, Isaac, and Jacob.

Joseph's brothers grow jealous (37:1-11):

Jacob continued to live in Canaan at Hebron (35:27; 37:14).

Joseph, at the age of seventeen, worked with his brothers caring for the sheep. As he worked with the sons of Bilhah and Zilpah, he brought his father a bad report about them, indicating these sons were engaged in evil deeds.

Israel loved Joseph more than all his other sons because he was the son of his old age, and he showed his partiality by making a coat of many colors for him. When Joseph's brothers saw that their father loved Joseph more than he loved them, they hated him and could not even greet him in a pleasant tone.

To make matters worse, Joseph dreamed a dream which he told to his brothers: "Let me tell you a dream I have had. We were binding bundles of wheat in the field, and my bundle stood up straight, and your bundles all gathered around mine and bowed to it."

His brothers replied, "Do you think that you are going to rule over us?" And they hated him even more because of his dreams.

He dreamed a second dream and told them about it. "I dreamed that the sun, the moon, and eleven stars all bowed down to me."

When he told the dream to his father, Jacob rebuked him saying, "What kind of dream is this? Surely you do not think that I and your mother, and your brothers will bow before you." His brothers were jealous of him, but Joseph's father remembered the matter.

Joseph was born after all Jacob's other sons except Benjamin (30:27; 37:14). During the years between the birth of Joseph and the birth of Benjamin, Joseph would have appeared to be the last son Jacob would have, the son of his beloved wife Rachel, and this is what the expression, "son of his old age," means.

Word authorities say the expression "coat of many colors" comes from a word that means a coat reaching to the ankles and having long sleeves, in other words, a garment not designed for one to wear while doing manual labor. Since most Bible versions translate the expression as "a coat of many colors," and since there is no way for us to know exactly what it looked like, it is much better to go ahead with this description of the coat. The point is that the coat emphasized Jacob's partiality for Joseph.

Notice that there has now been an account of cruelty and violence on the part of Simeon and Levi; there has been an account of Reuben's fornication with Bilhah; and now Joseph reports evil actions on the part of the four sons of the concubines. Though it had not yet taken place, we have already looked at the story of Judah's sin with Tamar. No wonder Jacob loved a son who was so much more righteous than his other sons!

The site of ancient Dothan.

More and more children of today know very little, if anything, of modern methods of agriculture, and even less about ancient methods. For that matter, many or most adults know very little about such things. Learn enough and explain enough so that all will understand about sheaves of grain, but there is certainly no need to spend a class period on ancient farming methods.

Joseph is sold into slavery (37:12-36):

Joseph's brothers went to pasture their father's flock in Shechem. After they had been gone a while, Jacob told Joseph: "Your brothers are tending the flock in Shechem, are they not? Go and see if it is well with them and see how the flock is getting along." And he sent him from Hebron to Shechem.

When Joseph arrived at Shechem, he met a man in the field who asked him, "What are you looking for?" Joseph replied, "I am looking for my brothers. Can you tell me where they are?"

The man answered, "They have moved from here; for I heard them say, "Let us go to Dothan." So Joseph traveled the few miles northwest from Shechem to Dothan.

When Joseph's brothers saw him coming, they muttered to one another: "Here comes the dream master. Come, let's kill him and throw his body into one of these holes around here. We will tell our father that a wild animal killed him. Then we will see what becomes of his dreams."

But Reuben, the oldest, said, "Let's not actually kill him. Throw him into this pit out here in the wilderness and leave him, but don't kill him." Reuben pretended to be saying, "Let's cast him into this pit and leave him to die," but he was secretly planning to come back later and get him out and send him back to his father.

When Joseph reached them, therefore, they took his coat from him, and cast him into a dry hole. Then they calmly sat down to eat and ignored his cries (42:21).

After a time someone looked off into the distance and saw a caravan of Ishmaelites coming from Gilead on their way to Egypt with all kinds of spices. An idea occurred to Judah: "What profit is there if we kill our brother and hide his blood? Why don't we just sell him to these Ishmaelites? Then we won't have to kill him. After all, he is our brother." Judah's brothers all thought that was a good idea, so they pulled Joseph up out of the pit and sold him as a slave to be taken to Egypt. They received only twenty pieces of silver for their brother.

Reuben was not present when this transaction took place, so when he returned to the pit to find Joseph gone, he was very upset. He turned to his brothers and said, "The lad is gone; what am I going to do?"

In answer to their problem of finding an excuse for Joseph's absence, they killed a goat, and then dipped Joseph's coat in the blood. They sent the coat to their father with the message, "We found this coat. Is it Joseph's or not?"

Jacob immediately recognized the blood stained coat: "It is my son's coat. An awful beast has torn him to pieces and eaten him." For many days Jacob wore only clothes of mourning. When his sons and daughters came near to comfort him, he would not cheer up, but said, "I will mourn for my son till the day I die." So he wept for Joseph.

Meanwhile the Midianites sold Joseph to a man in Egypt named Potiphar, an officer of Pharaoh. Potiphar was chief of the executioners, that is, the commander of those who waited upon the king to execute sentence upon wrong-doers.

and it seems from this passage and others (compare with Judg. 6:3; 8:24) that the tribes had become one. It is to be expected that the names of these tribes would come to be used interchangeably for those whose appearance, lifestyle, and even ancestry, were so similar.

Map Assignment:

- Label Dothan on your map.
- Follow Joseph's route from Hebron, through Shechem, and on to Dothan.
- There were trade routes that came from Mesopotamia, through passes in Mount Carmel, and converged with the Way of the Sea to go on to the land of Egypt. Caravans of merchants, therefore, often passed through the land as they plied their trade from one country to another. And obviously, these brothers were feeding their sheep near enough to a trade route to see the caravan as it approached.

The price set by Moses for redeeming a slave who had been killed or disabled was thirty pieces of silver (Exod. 21:32), so the price for a strong young man should have been much higher. By purchasing Joseph for twenty pieces of silver, the traders could turn a nice profit on the venture. By selling Joseph for such a cheap price, the brothers demonstrated just how deep-seated their hatred of Joseph was. We can only dimly imagine the horror to Joseph, to be thus rudely taken from the bosom of a loving father, to face the hatred of his own brothers, and to be sold as a slave into a foreign land (42:21).

Three different terms are used in this chapter for the traders who were on their way to Egypt: Ishmaelites (37:25), Midianites (37:28), and Medanites (37:36—although most English translations have Midianites, the word is Medanites in the original language). Ishmael, Midian, and Medan were all sons of Abraham through his concubines (see 16:15; 25:2),

Joseph is betrayed by Potiphar's wife (39:1-23):

Jehovah blessed Joseph in the house of Potiphar so that everything he did prospered. When Potiphar observed how things under Joseph's care flourished, he turned his affairs over to him and made him overseer of all his estate. From that time on, the blessing of Jehovah was upon Potiphar's house and upon everything he had. Potiphar trusted Joseph so completely he did not concern himself over anything about his household, except for the food he ate.

Joseph was a pleasant, handsome young man. After a while Potiphar's wife began to look at Joseph with desire. She said to him, "Come to bed with me."

Joseph refused saying, "My master has put the greatest trust in me and has turned everything that is his over to me, except you, because you are his wife. How then could I do this great wickedness and sin against God?" Day after day she tried to get Joseph to commit adultery with her, but he would not. He even avoided being alone with her.

One day, Joseph came into the house to do his work, and no one else was there but Potiphar's wife. She caught hold of Joseph and said, "Come to bed with me." Promptly Joseph fled, but since she had hold of his outer coat, he pulled out of it to get away, and she was left holding the garment.

When she saw that he had left her holding his clothes and had run out, she called to the men of her house and said *(of Potiphar):* "See, he has brought in a Hebrew to show how little regard he has for us. This Hebrew came in to lie with me, but I cried out loud, and when he heard me cry out, he left his garment by me and fled." She kept the garment by her until Potiphar got home. Then she told him, "The Hebrew servant you brought to us came in to attack me, but when I cried out, he fled and left his garment."

Camels near the pyramids in Giza, Egypt.

When Potiphar heard the news, he was angry and he took Joseph and put him in the prison where the king's prisoners were kept.

Jehovah continued to be with Joseph even in prison and made him well regarded by the keeper of the prison. Soon the keeper placed the care and administration of the other prisoners under Joseph and whatever they did was in his hands. The keeper paid no attention to the affairs of the prisoners because Jehovah made everything prosper that Joseph did.

How easy it would have been for Joseph to give up his faith, to become a depressed, cynical person.

But he did not do so. Instead he was a diligent worker at whatever he did, and he never gave up his faith in God. Joseph is a splendid example to young people that the young can be strong—even in the face of severe trials and temptations.

Notice Joseph's answer when Potiphar's wife enticed him to sin with her. He said, "How then could I do this great evil, and sin against God?" It would have been a sin against her, against his master, against his own body—but ultimately all sin is against God He is the One offended by our sins, and He is the only One who can forgive. Joseph did not yield to the temptation.

Though it was a very sad day for Joseph to be accused and put in prison through no fault of his own, his punishment was extremely moderate for a slave accused of molesting his master's wife. It was so moderate that some wonder if Potiphar really was not deceived by his wife's story. Since, however, he had to accept either his wife's story or the word of a slave, he chose to punish Joseph to this degree. And though this act placed him on the bottom again, Joseph was now in position for the next step in God's plan. Once again, though cast down, Joseph did not give up his faith in God or become bitter. It is interesting that a little later, he, a slave and a prisoner with no hope of release, would ask the butler and baker, "Why are you depressed?" (40: 7).

Joseph interprets the dreams of the butler and the baker (40:1-23):

After a time the king of Egypt was offended by his butler *(the cupbearer who prepared the drinks for the king)* and by his baker *(the one who prepared the food for the king).* Pharaoh was so angry with these two officers he put them in the prison which was under the captain of the guard, the same prison where Joseph was kept. The captain placed the two prisoners in the personal care of Joseph.

One night both men dreamed dreams. The next morning, when Joseph came in and saw them, they were sad and dejected. He asked, "Why are you so depressed today?"

They answered, "We have each dreamed a dream, and there is no one to interpret it."

Joseph said, "Do not interpretations belong to God? Tell me your dreams, if you will?

The chief butler told his dream first: "In my dream, I saw a grape vine, and it had three branches. As I watched, it budded, then its blossoms shot forth, and the blossoms produced ripe grapes. I took Pharaoh's cup in my hand and squeezed the grapes into the cup and gave it to Pharaoh to drink?

Joseph said: "Here is what your dream means: The three branches are three days. In three days, Pharaoh will lift up your head and will restore you to your office, and you will serve Pharaoh as before. But please remember me when things are well with you again; remember the kindness I have shown to you, and mention me to Pharaoh and bring me out of this place. I was kidnaped out of the land of the Hebrews, and I have done nothing to deserve to be in this dungeon."

When the chief baker saw that the interpretation of the butler's dream was good, he said, "In my dream there were three baskets of fine bread on my head, and in the top basket there were all kinds of baked foods for Pharaoh. As I watched, the birds came and ate the goods from the basket."

Joseph told him, "Here is what your dream means: Within three days Pharaoh will lift up your head from off your shoulders and will hang your body on a stake, and the birds will eat your flesh."

Sure enough, on the third day, which was Pharaoh's birthday, he made a feast for all his servants. On the occasion, he restored the chief butler to his position, but he hanged the chief baker, just as Joseph had interpreted the dreams.

Nevertheless the chief butler did not remember Joseph, but forgot him.

As important officers under Pharaoh, these two men would have had access to the wise men who served the king. They would have been able to find someone to interpret their dreams if they had not been in prison, thus the depression.

Of all the bitter pills to swallow, for the butler whom he had befriended to forget him must been a difficult one for Joseph. He had excellent reason to believe that through the butler, he would gain access to the ear of Pharaoh. Expectations would have been high the first day or two, but after a week, and then a month, passed by, and there was no word, hope would have died. Still he kept his faith in God and his good attitude.

Pharaoh dreams (41:1-45):

Two more years passed. Then one night Pharaoh dreamed that he stood by the river *(the Nile)* and saw seven fat cows come up out of the river. These cows were healthy, nice-looking cows, and they fed on the reed-grass. As he watched, seven skinny, ugly cows came up out of the river and stood by the first cows—and the seven lean cows proceeded to eat the seven fat cows! Pharaoh woke up.

He went back to sleep and dreamed again. He saw a stalk of grain, and there were seven well-filled ears of grain on the one stalk. Then came another stalk with seven ears which were thin and dried by the east wind, and the seven lean ears ate up the seven fat ones.

The next morning Pharaoh was very worried, and he could not get the dreams out of his mind. He called in all the sacred scribes and wise men of Egypt, but none of them could tell him what his dreams meant.

The chief butler finally spoke: "I will make mention of my faults today. One time Pharaoh was angry with his servants and put me and the chief baker in the custody of the captain of the guards. We each dreamed a dream in the night, and there was a young man, a Hebrew, a slave of the captain of the guard, and we told him our dreams, and he interpreted them, and his interpretations came true. Just as he said, I was restored to my office and the chief baker was hanged."

Pharaoh called for Joseph immediately. As soon as Joseph was summoned, he shaved, changed into different clothes, and came in before Pharaoh. The king said, "I have dreamed a dream, and no one can interpret it. I have heard that you can interpret dreams."

Joseph answered, "It is not in me, but God will give Pharaoh a favorable answer." Pharaoh proceeded to tell Joseph his dreams. When he finished, Joseph said:

> The message of Pharaoh's two dreams is one message. God has told Pharaoh what He is about to do. The seven good cows and the seven good ears are seven years. The seven skinny cows and the seven bad ears of grain are also seven years. The meaning is that there will come seven years of great plenty throughout the land of Egypt, and after them will arise seven years of famine during which all the plenty shall be forgotten, and the famine will consume the land. The dream has been doubled because it is established by God and will surely come to pass.

> Therefore let Pharaoh find a man who is prudent and wise and set him over the land of Egypt. Also let him appoint overseers and let them see that the fifth part of the harvest is put aside during the years of plenty. In that way, food will be stored up during the years of plenty for the years of famine which will come, so that the land will not perish during the famine.

Joseph's advice was very well taken by Pharaoh, and he said to his servants, "Where can we find another like this man, in whom is the spirit of Elohim?" Turning to Joseph he said, "Since God Himself has shown you this, there is no one so prudent and wise as you. You will be over my affairs, and my people will be governed according to your word. Only on the throne will I be greater than you."

Pharaoh took off his signet ring by which the official stamp of Pharaoh was given, and put it on Joseph's hand. He said, "See, I have hereby set you over the land of Egypt." He clothed Joseph in garments of fine linen, and put a gold necklace around his neck. He gave orders for him to ride in Pharaoh's second chariot, and they proclaimed before him, "Bow the knee!" Pharaoh said, "Though I am Pharaoh, yet without your permission, no one shall raise a hand or a foot in all Egypt." He gave Joseph an Egyptian name, Zaphenath-paneah, which means "Sustainer of Life" or "Preserver of Life." And he gave him a wife named Asenath, the daughter of the priest of On (*Heliopolis, located perhaps twenty miles north of Memphis, at the very base of the Nile Delta*).

Thus Joseph went out over the land of Egypt.

Joseph is ruler in Egypt (41:46-57):

Joseph was thirty years old when he stood before Pharaoh and became ruler over all the land of Egypt. As Joseph had predicted, for the next seven years, the earth brought forth by handfuls, and Joseph stored up all the extra food from the fields which were around every city. So much grain was stored that all attempts at keeping accurate records were abandoned.

During these seven years, two sons were born to Joseph by his wife Asenath, daughter of Potiphera (*which means, "consecrated to the sun"*). The firstborn was named Manasseh (*"naking to forget"*) because Joseph said, "God has made me forget all my toil, and all my father's house," or as we would say, "God has helped me to get over my years of slavery and the loss of my association with my family." The name of the second son was Ephraim (*to be fruitful'*) because he said, "God has made me fruitful in the land of my hardships."

The seven years of plenty ended, and the seven years of famine began. There was famine in all the lands around Egypt, but only in Egypt was there bread. As the effects of the famine grew in the land of Egypt, the people cried to Pharaoh for help. He told them, "Go to Joseph; whatever he tells you, do." So Joseph opened the storehouses and sold grain to the Egyptians. Furthermore, people from all countries around came to Egypt to buy grain from Joseph because the famine was severe everywhere.

Circumstances have now made it inevitable that Joseph's family would come to Egypt. It is truly fascinating to behold the unfolding of God's plan here. It illustrates how men may fit into God's plan without realizing what part they are playing until the plan comes to fruition.

Chronology Note

- *Joseph was seventeen when the story about his brothers' jealousy begins (37:2).*

- *Now when he stands before Pharaoh and is made ruler of Egypt, he is 30 years old (41:46).*

- *That means thirteen years passed while Joseph was first a slave in Potiphar's house and then was in prison.*

- *Before the brothers come to Egypt, the seven years of plenty have passed and the years of famine have begun.*

- *That means Joseph was more than 37 years old when the brothers first bowed before him.*

Joseph's brothers come to buy grain (42:1-38):

Jacob learned there was grain in Egypt, and he said to his sons, "Why are you just looking at one another? I have heard there is grain in Egypt. Go there and buy some for us lest we die." So Joseph's ten older brothers traveled to Egypt to buy grain. Jacob would not permit Benjamin to go, however, because he said, "Something bad might happen to him."

So it was that Jacob's sons were among those who came from other countries to buy grain in Egypt. And Joseph was the governor of all Egypt! Joseph recognized his brothers immediately, but he played his role as the governor and spoke roughly to them. "Where are you from?" he demanded.

"From the land of Canaan to buy food," the brothers answered, not thinking in their wildest dreams that this man could be the brother they sold so long ago.

As he observed his brothers bowing before him, Joseph vividly remembered the dream he had as a boy. He said, "You are spies. You have come to study the weaknesses of our land."

"No, my lord. We have come merely to buy food. We are all sons of one man. We are sincere men, not spies."

"No, you have come to spy out the defenseless condition of the land," Joseph replied.

"We, your servants, are twelve brothers, the sons of one man in the land of Canaan. The youngest is with our father, and one is no more."

Joseph answered, "I have charged you with being spies: in this way you will be tested. By the life of Pharaoh, you will not leave here unless your younger brother comes. Send one of you to go get your brother, but the rest of you will be bound. This way we will know whether you are spies or not," and he put them all in prison for three days.

After the three days, Joseph said to them, "Do this and live. I fear God, so if you are indeed sincere men, let one of your brothers be bound and left here while the rest of you carry grain for the famine to your families who are suffering. Then bring your youngest brother to me, and your words will be proven, and you won't die."

In deep distress, the brothers said to one another: "We are truly guilty over what we did to our brother, because we saw his anguish and yet would not listen to him. That is why we are having this trouble." Reuben said, "Didn't I tell you not to sin against the boy, and you wouldn't listen? God is paying us back."

Joseph had been using an interpreter so the brothers did not know he understood what they were saying, but he was moved to tears by their words and turned away to weep. When he returned, he took Simeon from among them and bound him as they watched. Then Joseph commanded that their vessels be filled with grain and that every man's money be put back in his sack, and also that extra provisions be given them for their journey.

As the brothers were on their way home, one of them opened a grain sack to feed the donkeys, and he found the money they had paid for the grain. He said to the rest, "My money has been given back. It is right here in my sack."

At this they were frightened and said, "What has God done to us?"

When they arrived home they told their father all that had happened: "The man, the lord of the country, spoke harshly to us; he thought we were spies of the country. But we told him, 'We are honest men, twelve brothers, sons of our father, but one is no more, and the youngest is with our father today in Canaan.' He told us, 'By this I shall know that you are honest men: leave one of your brothers with me and take grain for your families and go. But you must bring your youngest brother with you so that I can know you are telling the truth and are not spies. Then I will restore your brother Simeon to you and you may trade freely in the land.'"

As each one emptied his sack, they discovered that all of them had their money returned, and they were very afraid. Jacob was very upset and said, "You have bereaved me of my children. Joseph is gone, Simeon is gone, and you would take Benjamin away. All these things are against me."

Reuben said to his father, "Kill my two sons if I do not bring him back to you. Put him into my care and I will bring him back to you."

But Jacob answered, "My son will not go down with you. His brother is dead, and he only is left *(of his mother)*. If something happened to him on the trip, then you would bring my gray head to Sheol *(the grave)* in sorrow."

Joseph knew of the effects of the famine in other lands, so it had surely occurred to him that his brothers, or someone from the family, would come to buy grain. Yet he must have felt a degree of shock to see his brothers bowing before him with their faces to the ground—and to realize how completely his dream of the sheaves of wheat bowing to his had come true. (37:5-7)

The Bible does not tell why Simeon was the one chosen to be kept as a prisoner while the others went home, but it is interesting to do a little speculating based on the facts given.

- *Reuben was the oldest and therefore the one most likely to be held responsible for the actions of the brothers.*

- *But it was not the oldest that Joseph kept.*

- *This was the first time he learned that Reuben had tried to spare his life all those years ago, because he had not yet arrived when Reuben suggested they put him in the pit rather than kill him, and he was already gone with the band of merchants on his way to Egypt when Reuben came back to find the lad gone and protested to his brothers(37:21-22, 28-30).*

- *Almost certainly that is why Joseph wept, and why he chose the second oldest as the one to keep.*

The brothers return to Egypt (43:1-14):

Time passed, the famine continued as severe as ever, and the grain from Egypt was gone, so Jacob told his sons, "Go again, buy us a little food."

This time it was Judah who reasoned with his father. "The man told us in all seriousness that we would not even see him if we don't bring Benjamin. If you send our brother with us, we will go and buy food, but if not, we will not go. It would be useless if the governor will not see us, and he will refuse unless our brother is with us."

Jacob cried out in frustration, "Why did you treat me so badly as to tell him you had a brother?"

The brothers replied, "The man asked specifically about us and our kindred. He said, 'Is your father alive? Do you have another brother?' And we answered him. How could we know he would say, 'Bring your brother down'?"

Judah said, "Send the young man with me and we will go down so that we can all live, we as well as you and our little ones. I will guarantee his return. If I don't bring him back to you, then let me bear the blame forever. If we had not delayed, we would already have returned twice."

Seeing that he had no choice, Jacob said, "If it must be so, do this: take some nice gifts from the land here, a little balm, some honey, spices and myrrh, pistachio nuts and almonds. Take double the amount of money necessary, plus the money that was returned. Maybe it was an oversight. Take your brother also and go again to the man, and may God Almighty give you mercy in the eyes of the man so that he will release to you your other brother and Benjamin. And if I am bereaved of my children, I am bereaved."

So the brothers gathered the present for the governor, took their money, and Benjamin, and returned to Egypt to stand before Joseph.

It was not that Judah made a better plea to his father than Reuben had made earlier; it was the time factor that made the difference. Reuben made his offer very soon after they had returned with the grain the first time, and Jacob refused his suggestion. By now, however, the food is giving out, and necessity makes Jacob listen to their reasoning.

The brothers dine with Joseph (43:16-34):

Joseph saw that Benjamin was with the brothers before he spoke with them. He told his steward, "Bring the men to my house and prepare a feast because they will eat with me at noon."

When the steward took Joseph's brothers to his house, they were afraid and thought something was badly wrong. "It is because of the money that was returned in our sacks the first time we were here. He is setting us up to get us in trouble, to take what we have and make us slaves."

To prevent the trouble they feared, the brothers spoke to the steward, saying, "O, my lord, the first time we came to buy food, on our way home, when we opened our grain sacks, behold, each man's money was in the mouth of his sack. So we have brought it back. We have also brought additional money with us to buy food this time. We do not know who put our money back into our sacks."

Ancient Egyptian ruins from Edfu, Egypt.

The steward said, "Don't worry about it. Do not be afraid. Your God, the God of your fathers, has given you treasure in your sacks; I had your money."

After bringing Simeon to them, the steward gave them all water to wash their feet, and he saw that their donkeys were fed. Meanwhile, everything was being prepared for the feast at noon. By now the brothers had learned they were to eat at Joseph's house, so they prepared their present to give to him.

When Joseph arrived, the brothers bowed themselves low before him and presented their offering. Joseph asked how they were and said, "Is your father well, the old man you told me about?"

"Your servant our father is well; he is still alive," they replied, bowing still in homage.

Then Joseph looked at Benjamin and, realizing that this was his full brother, his mother's other son, he said, "Is this your youngest brother you told me about?" He said to Benjamin, "I hope God will be gracious to you, my son." Then Joseph hurried to his chamber *(probably his bedroom)* because his emotions arose in his heart, and he had to find a place where he could weep.

Look back to the chronology note on page 99. Remember that Benjamin would have been no more than a very young child when Joseph had last seen him, but now he is old enough to have ten children (46:21). What a poignant moment!

After a time, Joseph washed his face and controlled himself, and said to his servants, "Serve the meal."

Joseph ate at a table alone, as befitted the dignity of his position as ruler; the Egyptians who ate with him ate at another table; and his brothers ate at still a third table. The Egyptians would not eat with Joseph's brothers because it was an abomination to them to eat with Hebrews.

The brothers of Joseph were seated according to age, from the firstborn down to the youngest. Joseph's brothers marveled with one another, wondering how this Egyptian governor could know their ages. During the meal, food was served from Joseph's table to each of the brothers, but Benjamin's serving was five times as much as any of the others. The meal was a pleasant one, with plenty to eat and drink for all.

Remember the ages of the brothers were much too close together for anyone to be able to tell their order just by observation. Name them by age to be sure you could have seated them.

The Hebrews, along with other Asiatic peoples, slaughtered their animals for food, including female animals. Female animals, however, were regarded as sacred by the Egyptians. Therefore the Egyptians did not eat with the Hebrews because the Hebrews might have slain a female animal and have been contaminated or unclean to the Egyptians (K & D., Vol. I, p. 277).

Notice one more part of God's plan for His people:

- *The people of Canaan would have been glad to mingle with this rich family and to become one with them.*

- *The Philistines around Gerar made a treaty of peace with Abraham (21:22-34) and then later with Isaac (26:26-33).*

- *The men of Shechem went out to request that they be allowed to become one with Jacob's family and even underwent the process of circumcision to try to be acceptable (34:8-24).*

- *So far as we know, all the sons of Jacob except Joseph married women of the land of Canaan.*

- *Yet, God wanted this family to develop into a distinct race, one that could be a separate nation unto Him.*

- *So events are developing that will take them into a land where the natives will not even eat with foreigners, much less become one people with them.*

Joseph tests his brothers (44:1-34):

By showing Benjamin obvious preference, Joseph was preparing a way to conduct a test of his brothers. He gave his steward instructions: "Fill every man's sack full, as much as he can carry, and put every man's money into his sack's mouth. Put my cup, the silver cup, in the mouth of the sack that belongs to the youngest, along with his grain money." The steward followed Joseph's instructions exactly.

Next morning, as soon as it was light, the brothers were on their way. They must have been leaving Egypt with their hearts light: Benjamin was safe; Simeon was safe; the governor had been friendly rather than harsh this time; all had gone well. They were not far out of the city, however, when everything changed. The steward, following further instructions from Joseph, overtook them and said, "Why have you returned evil to my master when he did you good? Is not this cup the one from which my lord drinks and by which he foretells the future? How could you do such a thing?"

The brothers were shocked and said, "Why do you make such accusations against us? We would not do such a thing. We brought back the money we found in our grain sacks. Would we do that if we were the type to steal? If you find the cup on any one of us, let him be put to death, and we will be slaves to your master."

The servant said, "Let it be as you have said, except that whoever has the cup will be my lord's slave, and the rest of you will be free."

Hurriedly, the sacks were taken from the donkeys and placed on the ground, and every sack was untied. The steward began searching with the sack of Reuben and searched each man's sack, beginning with the oldest and going to the youngest, until he came to the sack of Benjamin—ten sacks with no silver cup! By this time, the brothers were probably feeling smug and more than a little indignant. Then the steward pulled the cup out of Benjamin's sack! Of course, none of the brothers, and Benjamin least of all, knew how the cup had gotten into the sack. They were devastated; they rent their clothes, loaded the grain back on the donkeys, and returned to the city.

The crux of Joseph's test was to see if the brothers were jealous of Benjamin as they had been of him. If they were, and wished to get rid of Benjamin, Joseph gave them a perfect opportunity to do so. But the brothers were changed men. They still remembered Joseph's anguish; they had seen their father grieve through the years; and they were unwilling to treat Benjamin as they had Joseph.

When Judah and his brethren returned to Joseph's house, he was still there, and they fell before him on the ground *(remember the dream?)*. Joseph said, "How could you do such a deed? Did you not know that a man such as I has the power to know what men do?"

Judah answered, "What shall we say? We have no way to clear ourselves. God has uncovered our iniquity. We

Statue of an Egyptian pharaoh.

are your slaves, both we and the one who had your cup in his possession."

Joseph replied, "O, far be it from me to keep you all. No, I will keep only the guilty one. The rest of you can go in peace to your father."

Then Judah came closer to Joseph and said:

O, my lord, let me say a few words for you to ponder, and I hope you will not be angry, because you are equal to Pharaoh. You asked if we had a father or a brother when we were here the first time. We told you that we had a father, an old man, and a child of his old age, just a young fellow. "His brother is dead," we said, "and he is the only child left of his mother, and his father loves him."

Then you said to us, "Bring him down to me, so that I can see him." But we told you that the lad could not leave his father because, if he did, his father would die. But you said, "Unless your youngest brother comes down, you will not be allowed to see me."

When we returned home, we told our father what you said. After a while our father said, "Go again, buy us a little food." But we said, "We cannot go down; if you let Benjamin go with us, then we will go; if not, there is no point in going because we will not be able to see the man."

Our father answered, "You know my wife gave me two sons. One I have lost, apparently torn to pieces, and if you take this one also, and something bad happens to him, you will bring my gray hairs down to Sheol *(the grave)*."

You see, I became surety for the lad. I said, "If I do not bring him back to you, then I will

bear the blame forever." Therefore, I beg you, let me remain with you as your slave, and let the lad return to his father. How can I go back to my father if the lad is not with me? I could not stand to see the calamity and grief of my father if I did such a thing.

Joseph reveals himself to his brothers (45:1-15):

When Judah made this emotional speech, Joseph could restrain himself no longer. He ordered everyone out of the room but his brothers. Then he gave vent to the pent-up emotions of twenty-two years and wept aloud. He wept so loudly the Egyptians outside the room heard—and the whole house of Pharaoh heard the news quickly.

Joseph said, "I am Joseph. Does my father still live?" But his brothers were absolutely stunned, unable to speak because of his presence.

He said to them, "Come near, please." They came closer and he said, "I am Joseph your brother whom you sold into Egypt. Don't be grieved or angry with yourselves because you sold me here. It was God who sent me before you to preserve life. This famine has been upon the land two years, and five more years remain. God has sent me before you to save you, and He has made me a provider for Pharaoh and a ruler over all the land of Egypt. Hurry home, therefore, and tell my father, this is what your son Joseph says: "God has made me lord of all Egypt. Come down to me without delay. You will dwell in the land of Goshen, and you will be with me, you and your children and your grandchildren and your flocks and herds and everything you have. I will nourish you because there are still five years of famine.' You and Benjamin can see for yourselves that it is really I who speaks to you. Tell my father of all my glory in Egypt, and hurry and bring him here."

Joseph hugged Benjamin and wept. Then he kissed all his brothers and wept. Afterward, his brothers talked with him.

Here when Joseph has just told his brothers who he is, and that he wants the family to come to Egypt, he tells them they can live in Goshen, one of the very best parts of the land. This means that Joseph had been hoping for this eventuality. He had been planning how he could provide for his father and for his whole family.

Do you remember that it was Judah who suggested that they sell Joseph to the merchants (37:26)? Now it is Judah who offers himself as a slave in Benjamin's place.

Chronology Note

This is one more passage that helps us know how long Joseph had been in Egypt.

- *He was 30 when he stood before Pharaoh and interpreted his dreams (41:46).*

- *Then seven years of plenty came and went (41:46-52).*

- *By now, 45:6, there have been two years of famine in the land, and there are five more years to go.*

- *Seven years of plenty, plus two years of famine, equal nine years since Joseph became ruler of Egypt. This means he was 39 years old when he sent for his father.*

- *But he was only 17 when he was sold (37:2), so it has been 22 years since he saw his father.*

Preparations for Israel to move to Egypt (45:16-28):

When Pharaoh heard the news that Joseph's family had arrived, he was very pleased and he told Joseph to tell his brothers to go to Canaan and get his father and all his family and bring them to Egypt. Pharaoh said, "I will give you the best of the land of Egypt, and you will have everything you need. Take wagons from Egypt for your children and for your wives. Do not worry about your household goods because the best of everything in Egypt is yours."

Joseph's brothers did as they were told and took wagons. Pharaoh gave them supplies for their journey. He also gave them changes of clothes, but to Benjamin he gave three hundred pieces of silver and five changes of clothes. To Jacob he sent ten donkeys loaded with good things from Egypt and ten more loaded with grain and bread and other provisions for their journey. Joseph sent them off with the warning not to quarrel on the way.

The brothers made their way back to Canaan, and they rushed in to tell Jacob, "Joseph is yet alive, and he is ruler over all the land of Egypt." Jacob fainted, not able to believe what they were saying. But they told him all Joseph had said, and he saw the wagons Joseph had sent. So Jacob took heart and said, "It is enough: Joseph my son is still alive, and I will go and see him before I die."

Israel moves to Egypt (46:1-27):

Leaving Hebron (35:27), Jacob came to Beersheba, the point of departure from Canaan to go to Egypt. There he offered sacrifices unto the God of his father Isaac. God appeared to Israel that night and told him, "I am God, the God of your father. Fear not to go down into Egypt because there I will make of you a great nation. I will be with you and I will surely bring you up again. And when you die, Joseph will be there to close your eyes."

Promise repeated here: Nation

Jacob arose, and his sons carried their father, their children, and their wives in the wagons Pharaoh had provided. They brought all their cattle and their goods into Egypt.

In Genesis 46:8-27 the family of Jacob is listed. The family is grouped under the mothers:

- Leah's children: Reuben, Simeon, Levi, Judah, Issachar, and Zebulun, are listed along with their children. A total of 33 are named including Er and Onan, who died in Canaan before the move to Egypt.

- Zilpah's children and grandchildren are listed with a total of sixteen.

- Rachel's children and grandchildren are listed with a total of fourteen.

- Finally, seven children and grandchildren are counted for Bilhah.

- These figures yield a total of seventy.

There are variations in the figures given for the number of people in the family at this time. Look at these points and explanations:

- *Er and Onan died in Canaan, but if they are not counted in the total, there are 31 descendants of Leah instead of 33, with an overall total of 68 instead of 70. Obviously, then, Er and Onan are included in the total of 70.*

- *In 46:26, the figure for the total is 66. The best explanation is that 66 is the number of Jacob's family, not counting himself, or Joseph and his two sons. Counting them in, we have the figure 70.*

- *Stephen speaks of 75 (Acts 7:14). He uses the LXX (Septuagint) version which says 75 in this passage. To the words found in our common translations of 46:20, the LXX adds these words: "And there were sons born to Manasseh, which the Syrian concubine bore to him, even Machir. And Machir beget Galaad. And the sons of Ephraim, the brother of Manasseh: Sutalaam, and Taam. And the sons of Sutalaam: Edom. "This passage adds five names. Consequently, the LXX gives the number 75 in 46:27 rather than 70. The information was probably added by the LXX translators from Numbers 26:29, 35-36 (in the LXX, Num. 26:33, 39-40) in order to be consistent, naming all sons and grandsons of Jacob.*

- *Whether the exact figure was 66, 70, or 75, it was a large family by this time, but still a long way from being a nation of people.*

The Nile Delta, where the land of Goshen was located.

Joseph introduces his family to Pharaoh (47:1-12):

Joseph went in before Pharaoh and said, "My family has come from Canaan and they are presently in the land of Goshen." With him, Joseph had five of his brothers, and he presented them to Pharaoh. Pharaoh asked, "What is your occupation?"

They said, "We are shepherds, both we and our ancestors. We have come to stay for a while in Egypt because there is no pasture for our flocks in Canaan. We would like to have permission to live in the land of Goshen."

Jacob and Joseph are re-united (46:28-34):

As they approached Egypt, Jacob sent Judah ahead to get directions from Joseph to the land of Goshen.

When Joseph learned they had arrived, he made his chariot ready and went out to meet Israel his father at Goshen. He presented himself to him and hugged his father and wept a good while.

Israel said to Joseph, "Now let me die, since I have seen your face and know you are alive."

Joseph told his father and his brothers: "I will go to Pharaoh, and I will say, 'My brothers and my father's whole family have come to me. They are shepherds and keepers of cattle, and they have brought their flocks and their herds.' Then when Pharaoh asks you what is your occupation, you will say to him, 'We have been shepherds all of our lives, both we and our forefathers.' In that way you will be able to live in the land of Goshen, because every shepherd is an abomination to the Egyptians."

Again God's providence is at work. By placing Israel's family in a distinct section of the land, and by their occupation being one that was an abomination to the Egyptians, they will tend to stay separate from the other inhabitants of the land. They will become the distinct, separate nation God wants.

Pharaoh replied, speaking to Joseph: "Your family has come, and the land of Egypt is before you. Let them live in the best part of the land; let them stay in Goshen, and if you know any diligent men among them, then put them in charge of my cattle."

Joseph brought in his father Jacob and presented him to Pharaoh, and Jacob blessed the ruler. Pharaoh asked Jacob, "How long have you lived?"

Jacob answered, "The years of my pilgrimage are 130 years. Few and hard have my years been, and I have not lived as long as my ancestors did during their pilgrimages." So Jacob blessed Pharaoh and left his presence.

According to the permission Joseph had received from Pharaoh, he placed Israel's family in Goshen near Rameses, and he provided food for all his brothers and for their families.

Abraham lived to be 175, and Isaac, 180. The Hebrew writer refers to this passage as he declares that the patriarchs confessed that "they were strangers and pilgrims on the earth" (Heb. 11:9, 13-16).

Jacob's description of his life is vivid: "Few and evil have the days of my life been..." Since he had only lived 130 years, there had not yet been time for him to live as long as his father and grandfather, but he is correct that he does not live as long as they. We will come to the story of his death soon.

The city of Rameses was adjacent to the city of Tanis or Zoan. It has been widely assumed that since Rameses (or Raamses) was built by the Israelites (Exod. 1:11), that the Pharaoh of the Exodus was Rameses II. The reign of Rameses II is, however, dated 1290-1224. The date of his reign does not fit at all with Bible statements regarding the time of the Exodus (see 1 Kings 6:1, e.g.). The mention of Rameses in Genesis 47:11 indicates there must have been a city by that name earlier than Israel's slavery, and that it was rebuilt or enlarged by the Israelites in the early days of the book of Exodus.

If the Raamses of Exodus 1:11 were built under Rameses II, then it was a later Pharaoh who ruled at the time of the Exodus because the first Pharaoh mentioned in the book of Exodus died before the Exodus occurred (Exod. 2:23). There is no conclusive evidence for a late date for the Exodus. The evidence in the Bible definitely points to an early date. We will look at that evidence more closely in the study of the book of Exodus.

Joseph purchases the land of Egypt for Pharaoh (47:13-26):

The famine continued unabated, and all the inhabitants of Egypt and Canaan languished because of it. Joseph continued to sell grain to the Egyptians until their money was all in the hands of Pharaoh. Then the people came to him and said, "Give us bread. Why should you watch us die? Our money is gone."

Joseph answered, "Give your cattle in exchange for grain if your money has run out." That year the people exchanged horses, flocks, and herds for bread.

The next year the people came and said, "Our money is spent, and our cattle belong to my lord; we have nothing left but our bodies and our land. Buy us and our land for bread. We and our land will be for the service of Pharaoh, and give us seed so that we can live and so the land will not be desolate."

Therefore Joseph bought all the land for Pharaoh. He resettled the people from one end of Egypt to the other. The land of the priests was not sold, however, because Pharaoh gave them a regular allowance. Joseph said to the people, "See, I have bought you this day and your land for Pharaoh. Now here is seed for you to plant. When you harvest your crops, you will give a fifth to Pharaoh. The other four parts will be your own, for seed and for food for your families."

The people were grateful and said, "You have saved our lives. We hope to please you, and we will serve Pharaoh."

Joseph made it a statute, which lasted until the days when this account was written, that Pharaoh's portion would be a fifth, except for the lands of the priests.

Several secular writers have borne witness that the people of Egypt did not own their land, but rented or leased it from Pharaoh. Herodotus, for example, says: Pharaoh "Sesotris also divided the land of Egypt in equal plots among the inhabitants. These paid dues for their land year by year, and so the King had his revenue" (Stories of the East From Herodotus, by Alfred J. Church, 138). Herodotus lived over a thousand years (484 to 425 BC) after Joseph bought the land for Pharaoh, so it seems the Egyptians continued the custom for many years.

Jacob's death draws near (47:27-31):

The Israelites continued to live in Goshen and grew in their possessions, and also multiplied exceedingly in number.

Jacob lived in Egypt seventeen years, so that he lived a total of 147 years. When the time drew near for him to die, Jacob called Joseph in to see him and said, "If I have found favor with you, please swear to me and promise you will deal kindly and truly with me. Do not bury me in Egypt. When I am dead, carry me out of Egypt and bury me with my ancestors."

Joseph said, "I will do as you have said."

Jacob replied, "Swear unto me," and Joseph swore to him. Then Jacob bowed himself (*in worship*) upon his *staff (or toward the head of the bed)*.

The LXX and some other versions have: "He bowed upon his staff." Some translations say: "And Israel bowed himself upon the bed's head." The writer of Hebrews, following the LXX, refers to Jacob blessing his sons, "Worshiping, leaning upon the top of his staff" (Heb. 11:21). The most reliable Hebrew text says "bed" instead of staff. Except for the Masoretic vowel signs, the words for staff and for bed are the same, but the vowel signs in the Masoretic text (which is the oldest complete Hebrew text in existence today) are for "bed." The primary point of the passage is that Jacob bowed here in worship as he is making this last request of his son Joseph.

Jacob blesses Ephraim and Manasseh (48:1-22):

After Jacob's burial arrangements were made, word came to Joseph that his father was sick. Joseph brought his two sons, Manasseh and Ephraim, to be blessed. Someone told Jacob, "Look, your son Joseph is coming," and Israel gathered his strength and sat up on his bed.

Jacob spoke to Joseph saying, "God Almighty appeared to me at Luz in the land of Canaan and blessed me and said to me, "I will multiply your descendants and will give this land to your seed after you for an ongoing possession." Now your two sons, who were born in Egypt before I came, are mine. Just as Reuben and Simeon, Ephraim and Manasseh will be my sons. Any further sons you have will be yours and will be considered a part either of Ephraim or Manasseh. To my sorrow Rachel died in the land of Canaan just a little distance from Ephrath, that is, Bethlehem."

> **Jacob bestows the birthright:**
>
> **Ephraim**
> **Manasseh**

Though Israel's eyes were dim with age, he could see the two sons of Joseph standing near, and he said, "Who are these?"

Joseph answered, "They are my two sons whom God has given me here."

"Bring them near, if you will, and I will bless them." Joseph brought his sons closer to the bed, and Jacob hugged them. Then he said, "I had given up all hope of ever seeing you again, and now God has let me see your sons also."

Joseph brought his sons out from Jacob's embrace and bowed with his face to the earth. Taking Manasseh on his left hand and Ephraim on his right hand, he moved them near to Jacob to receive the blessing—thus placing Manasseh the oldest on his father's right side. But as Israel reached out to lay his hands upon his grandsons, he crossed his hands so that his right hand was upon Ephraim, and his left was upon Manasseh. He said:

May the God before whom my fathers
Abraham and Isaac walked,
The God who has been my shepherd
all my life until this day,
The angel who has delivered me from all evil,
Bless these young men;
And may my name be named upon them,
And the names of my fathers,
Abraham and Isaac,
And let them grow to be a multitude
in the midst of the earth.

When Joseph saw that his father's right hand was upon Ephraim, and his left upon Manasseh his firstborn, he lifted his father's hands to move them and said, "No, Father, not that way, because this one is the firstborn. Put your right hand upon his head."

But Jacob refused, saying, "I know, my son, I know. He, too, will become a people, and he also will be great; however, his younger brother will be greater than he. His seed will become a multitude of nations." Jacob continued his blessing: "The day will come when the people of Israel will express a blessing by saying, 'May God make you to be as Ephraim and as Manasseh.'"

Then to Joseph himself Israel said, "I am dying, but God will be with you and will bring you again to the land of your ancestors. Moreover, I have given to you one portion of land more than your brothers which I took out of the hand of the Amorite with my sword and my bow."

Jacob was giving the birthright to Joseph as he blessed Joseph's two sons. Though Joseph was the eleventh son in line according to age, he was the oldest son of Jacob's beloved wife Rachel. Furthermore, there were reasons why Jacob would choose Joseph over the older sons as the one to inherit the birthright. Reuben had committed incest by going in unto Bilhah his father's wife. Therefore he was told he would no longer excel (49:3-4). First Chronicles 5:1 specifically says that it was Reuben's sin with Bilhah that kept him from receiving the birthright that would have been his. So Jacob gave it to Joseph instead. The tribes of Ephraim and Manasseh that will come through these two sons of Joseph were just as fully tribes as Reuben's, Simeon's, or any one of the others. Therefore Joseph received the birthright—a double portion of the inheritance, twice as much as the other brothers.

In the days of the Divided Kingdom, Ephraim's name became synonymous with the name of Israel, the northern kingdom. Ephraim was one of the predominant tribes even at the time of the conquest (Josh. 17:1418).

Jacob's language concerning the land he took with his sword and his bow is prophetic. In his lifetime, Jacob took no land from the Amorites. He purchased land (Gen. 33:19; Josh. 24:32), but he did not take any by conquest. Even the smiting of Shechem does not fit because it was an event that was totally against Jacob's wishes and one which he thoroughly repudiated (Gen.34:30; 49:5-7). Any violent taking of the land was ruled out by God for several generations in the days of Abraham when He said, "And in the fourth generation they shall come hither again: for the iniquity of the Amorites is not yet full" (15:16).

Therefore Jacob speaks prophetically of a thing which is to come as if it were an accomplished fact.

Jacob blesses his sons (49:1-28):

These blessings by the dying patriarch are prophetic. Most of them are clear enough, but with some of the blessings it is difficult to be certain exactly what was meant or specifically how they were fulfilled God keeps His promises, so we know everything was fulfilled just as God intended, but we do not have enough details to know exactly how in every case.

Jacob's words are expressed in poetic form, as is a great deal of the prophetic writing of the Bible. We are paraphrasing these prophecies, and then we sum up what is said and explain the historical references in connection with the prophecies that can be tied directly to some later bit of history.

Jacob called his sons together and said, "Gather together so that I may tell you the things which will happen to you in the future.

Gather together and hear, O sons of Jacob;
And listen to Israel your father.

The sons of Leah are blessed first.

Reuben—"Reuben, you are my first-born, the beginning of my strength. You could have had the first place in dignity and in power. But boiling over as water, you shall not have the first place, because you went up to your father's bed and defiled it."

Reuben was the firstborn son of Jacob. To him should have belonged the pre-eminence; but he was "unstable as water" or "boiling over as water." The latter translation is a more precise rendering of the original. The description refers to his uncontrolled desires and lusts which moved him to take Bilhah, his father's concubine (35:22). For this act he forfeited his birthright (1 Chron. 5:1).

Simeon and Levi—"Simeon and Levi are brothers, and their swords are tools of violence. Let me have nothing to do with their plans, because, provoked by anger, they killed men. Following their own ways, they crippled oxen. Cursed be their anger because it is fierce, and their wrath, for it is cruel.

I will divide them in Jacob and scatter them in Israel."

These two sons of Leah are joined together in the prophecy of Jacob because they acted together in the deed which brought shame upon Israel. The reference is to their smiting of the village of Shechem to avenge the seduction of Dinah their sister (chapter 34). Jacob pleads with his soul not to take part in their secret plan, which means that he utterly repudiated what they had done. As a consequence of their deed, Jacob declares that they would not be given a separate portion of the land, but were to be scattered through Israel.

Accordingly, when the Israelites went into the land and conquered it, five of the tribes, Reuben, Gad, Manasseh, Judah, and Ephraim, specifically asked for certain portions of the land and received their inheritance (Num. 32; Josh 13-17). Then there was a second round in which lots were cast between the rest of the tribes for the remaining territory. The second lot cast was for Simeon, and the Bible says, "Out of the part of the children of Judah was the inheritance of the children of Simeon" (Josh. 19:9). They were given cities in the southern part of Judah. Also, the tribe of Simeon did not multiply as much as did the children of Judah (see 1 Chron. 4:27). Later in Israelite history, some of the families of Simeon left their cities and went to a place called Gedor to the east of the land of Israel, while others moved to Mount Seir toward Edom (I Chron. 4:39-43).

The Levites were also scattered throughout Israel, but theirs turned out to be a position of great honor and service because they were chosen to be the priestly tribe (Exod 28:1). The Levites were not given a separate portion of land (Josh. 14:3-4), because the Lord was their inheritance. Instead they were given 48 cities, with the pasture lands that surrounded the

cities as their fields (Josh. 21:1-42; Num. 35:6).

Judah—"Judah, your brothers shall praise you; you shall conquer your enemies, and your father's sons shall bow down to you.

"Judah is a young lion. He leaves his prey to go lie down. Who will dare to rouse him up?

"The scepter shall not depart from Judah until Shiloh comes, and to Him shall the obedience of the peoples shall be.

"Tying his colt to the vine, he washes his garments in wine and his robes in the blood of grapes. His eyes shall be red with wine, and his teeth white from milk."

> ### A Messianic Promise to Judah: Genesis 49:10
>
> **The scepter shall not depart from Judah, nor the ruler's staff from between his feet until Shiloh come; and unto him shall the obedience of the peoples be.**

The last part of Jacob's prophecy to Judah probably refers to temporal blessings the tribe would enjoy in the land of Canaan. It became one of the richest and most prominent of the tribes. The temporal blessings were great, but the first part of the prophecy is of more relevance to the rest of the Bible story, so let us take time to notice that part carefully.

Judah's name means "Jehovah be praised" (29:35). Jacob tells Judah, "Your brothers will praise you. Your hand will be on the neck of your enemies; your brothers will bow down before you." Here the leadership and pre-eminence of Judah are specifically foretold. Judah's leadership was evident in the story of Joseph when he took the initiative in persuading his father to let Benjamin go to Egypt and in interceding with Joseph on behalf of Benjamin. In addition, during the travels in the wilderness, Judah's tribe led the way in their marching order (Num. 2:9). Most important, the family of David was of Judah, and through that line, through Judah and David, came the Christ.

The scepter shall not depart from Judah, nor the ruler's staff from between his feet until Shiloh come;

and unto him shall the obedience of the peoples be (Gen. 49:10). Take time to notice this part of the prophecy carefully, because of its Messianic nature. The scepter was the symbol of the right of a king to rule. Therefore, in prophecy, Jacob was saying the kings of Israel would be of Judah until Shiloh (the Prince of Peace) come. Shiloh was a city in Ephraim in the days of Israel. It was the city where the tabernacle was placed when the Israelites had conquered their enemies and were ready to make Canaan their own land (Josh. 18:1). The reference here, though, is not to the city of Shiloh. The city of Shiloh was in the territory of Ephraim and it had no more direct connection with Judah than it would have had to any other tribe. To escape the Messianic reference here, some have attempted to translate, "Till he (personifying the nation of Israel) come to Shiloh." But there were no kings in Judah before Israel came to the city of Shiloh. After the days of Eli, the city of Shiloh fell into ruins. Jeremiah refers to this fact when he says: "But go ye now unto my place which was in Shiloh, where I caused my name to dwell at the first, and see what I did to it for the wickedness of my people Israel" (Jer. 7:12). Therefore no sense can be made of

the prophecy if we attempt to apply it to the city of Shiloh.

Furthermore, when He who is Shiloh (Peace) appears, unto Him the obedience of the peoples will be given. Jesus is Shiloh (Peace). The rule of the Christ goes far beyond the confines of physical Israel. Indeed, unto Him has been given the obedience of the nations—"the peoples" (Psa. 2:8, 9). Among the Jews, Genesis 49:10 was regularly regarded as Messianic before the coming of Christ. Since Jesus came, however, Jews have forsaken the hope of a Messiah and seek to interpret Messianic passages in other ways. Their efforts make a travesty of Biblical interpretation.

Zebulun—"Zebulun shall dwell at the seashore and shall be a haven for ships. His flank shall be toward Sidon."

The words regarding Zebulun do not depict exact geographical location, because his territory did not extend to the Mediterranean or to the Sea of Galilee. His territory was in the northern half of the country, in the rich valley of Jezreel. His position made it possible for his tribe to enjoy the commerce of the sea and of Sidon (representing the whole country of the Phoenicians). Zebulun was not a prominent tribe in Israel, but in the song of Deborah, the tribe is commended for fighting along with the other tribes (Judg. 5:14, 18) It was the region of Zebulun and the area of Naphtali to the north that first suffered the ravages of the Assyrian king Tiglath-pileser III in the days when Israel was falling (2 Kings 15:29). Isaiah prophesies comfort to the region of Zebulun and Naphtali in the day when the Christ would come to do His great work in Galilee (Isa. 9:1-2; Matt. 4:13-16).

Issachar—"Issachar is a strong donkey lying down between the packs. When he saw that a resting place was good, he bowed his shoulders to carry burdens, and became a slave at forced labor."

Not much definite information can be drawn from this prophecy. Perhaps it indicates that Issachar would be content to do his work and would, therefore, not be willing to exert himself for the nation as a whole. He would thus prefer to submit to a role of slavery than to risk his peace in a struggle for free-

---

God has revealed this much of His plan for the scheme of redemption:

- A descendant of Eve will come who will defeat Satan (3:15).
- He will bless all families of the earth (12:3).
- He will reign—have a scepter (49:10).
- He will come through the line of Eve, through Abraham, through Isaac, through Jacob, and now through Judah.

There is still very little we know about this One who is to come, but we know much more than we did in the Garden of Eden when sin entered the world.

dom. If this interpretation is correct, it may explain why Issachar is the last of Leah's sons Jacob deals with in his prophetic statements. During the days of Deborah, however, the tribe of Issachar is praised because "the princes of Issachar were with Deborah; as was Issachar, so was Barak; into the valley they rushed forth at his feet" (Judg. 5:15). Issachar is never a prominent tribe.

The next four sons blessed were sons of the handmaids.

Dan—"Dan shall judge his people, as one of the tribes of Israel. He shall be a serpent in the road that bites the horse's heel and causes his rider to fall backwards. For thy salvation I wait, O Lord."

The name Dan means judged, "and Jacob's prophecy makes a play on the word. The meaning is that Dan would secure justice for his people, the tribes of Israel. How this prophecy is fulfilled is uncertain. Some suggest that it may have been fulfilled through the activities of Samson, whose family members were Danites (Judg. 13:2).

The latter part of the prophecy, about his being a serpent, may refer either to the activities of Dan recorded in Judges 17-18 as the tribe made a stolen idol its god, and/or the building of a shrine for the golden calf at the city of Dan in the days of Jeroboam I (1 Kings 12:28-30). In both incidences, Dan became a snare, a source of temptation to Israel, one who bites the heel to bring the rider down.

Gad—"A marauding band shall attack Gad, but he shall chase them away at their heels."

Gad was one of the tribes to inherit land in Transjordan. The prophecy to him probably applies to the constant pressure he would face from desert tribes pressing in upon Gilead and the valor with which he would thrust them back.

Asher—"As for Asher, his food shall be bountiful, and he shall yield royal dainties."

Asher's territory was one of the most fertile parts of Canaan and would contribute heavily to royal levies of food and produce.

Naphtali—"Naphtali is a deer set free; he gives beautiful words."

Perhaps the relative liberty Naphtali enjoyed in his territorial possession is the idea Jacob was predicting, but we have very little detail to go on. Naphtali was never a prominent tribe in Israel. Naphtali was joined with Zebulun in the ravages Tiglath-pileser III brought upon the land in his early raids, and as Isaiah gave his comfort to the territory in his predictions about the great light that would shine there in the days of the Messiah (2 Kings 15:29; Isa. 9:1-2; Matt. 4:13-16). Naphtali inherited the territory closest to the Sea of Galilee—the exact area where Jesus spent a major portion of His ministry in New Testament days.

Last Jacob gives blessings to the two sons of his favorite wife, Rachel.

Joseph—"Joseph is the son of a fruitful tree, a fruitful tree planted by a spring. Its branches run over the wall.

"The archers bitterly attacked him, and shot at him, and harassed him, but he could still draw his bow by the help of the Mighty One of Jacob (from there is the Shepherd, the Stone of Israel). The God of his father helps you, and the Almighty blesses you with blessings from heaven above and with blessings of the deep, blessings of the breasts and of the womb.

"The blessings of your father have surpassed the blessings of my ancestors, reaching as high as the very tops of the everlasting hills; may such blessings be upon the head of Joseph, and on the crown of the head of the one who is distinguished among his brothers?

More verses are devoted to Joseph than to any other son. By this the grateful love of Jacob for his beloved firstborn of Rachel is shown. He compares him to a fruit tree planted by a fountain of water. Joseph himself suffered much adversity, and he received his strength to overcome from God Almighty, but Jacob's message seems to point to the future struggles that Joseph's descendants would face. His help will come through "The Mighty One of Jacob," from "the Shepherd, the Stone of Israel," from the God of Joseph's father, and from the "Almighty."

Jacob notes that his blessings had surpassed those of his ancestors and he prays that such blessings will come to Joseph (and probably through him upon his descendants). Joseph is the one distinguished among his brethren by his sterling character and by his accomplishments in behalf of the family.

Notice very carefully that though Joseph is blessed so beautifully by his father, and though he received the birthright by his sons Manasseh and Ephraim being made tribes equivalent to the sons of Jacob, he is not the one given the promise of the Messiah. That promise went to Judah.

Benjamin—"Benjamin is a ravenous wolf; in the morning he devours the prey, and in the evening he divides the booty."

According to Jacob's prophecy, the men of Benjamin would show themselves to be warlike and very adept at warfare. Morning and evening would find them devouring their prey and dividing the spoils of their conquests. This figure points to their constant readiness to fight. This prophecy finds ample fulfillment in the history of the tribe. Ehud the judge sprang from Benjamin (Judg. 3:15). Benjamin took on all the other tribes in battle over the sins of the men of Gibeah (Judg. 19-21). And Saul and his great warrior son Jonathan were of Benjamin (1 Sam. 9:1). There are also several passages setting forth the prowess of the Benjamites in battle (Judg. 20:16; 1 Chron. 12:1-2).

The death of Jacob (49:29-33):

When Jacob finished blessing his sons, he said, "I am about to die. Bury me with my fathers in

Cave near the "Tomb of the Patriarchs" in Hebron.

the Cave of Machpelah in the field of Ephron the Hittite, which Abraham bought for a burial place. There they buried Abraham and his wife Sarah; there they buried Isaac and Rebekah; and there I buried Leah." When Jacob finished saying these things, he lay back, lifted his feet back onto his bed and died.

The embalming and burial of Jacob (50:1-14):

Joseph embraced the dead body of his father and wept over him and kissed him. Then he commanded his servants the physicians to embalm his father. The time required for the embalming was forty days. The Egyptians themselves mourned for Jacob for seventy days.

When the days of weeping were past, Joseph went to Pharaoh and said, "If I have pleased you, grant me a favor. My father made me swear that I would bury him in the land of Canaan. Therefore, please let me go and bury my father, and I will return."

Pharaoh gave his permission and sent a great host of Egyptian dignitaries to Canaan with the family. Joseph and the other members of Jacob's family, except the children, went up with chariots and cavalry; it was a very large group. They came up the east side of the Jordan to a place called the threshing floor of Atad and made a great lamentation for Jacob that lasted seven days. When the Canaanites saw the great procession of Egyptians, and heard their lamentations, they said, "This is a serious lamentation (ebel) to the Egyptians? Therefore they called the place Abel-mizraim.

Joseph and his brothers took the body of their father to Hebron and buried it in the Cave of Machpelah, just as he had promised. Then they returned to Egypt along with everyone else who had come with them.

Embalming was an art of the Egyptians that grew out of the demands of their religion. It was an effort to preserve the body as nearly intact as possible for their afterlife. There were different levels of embalming requiring different amounts of money and time. Jacob's was the more thorough embalming. The softer, more perishable, body parts were removed and replaced with preservatives. The body itself was soaked in preservatives and wrapped in cloths of linen. The bodies thus preserved would last almost indefinitely.

The name "Mizraim" was another name for Egypt. The Canaanites named the place "the weeping place of the Egyptians."

Joseph assures his brothers (50:15-21):

Now that Jacob was dead, the brothers of Joseph said to one another, "It may be that now Joseph will hate us and will repay us for all the evil we did to him? So they sent a message to Joseph which said, "Your father gave us a command before he died that we should ask you to forgive us of our transgression. We ask you, therefore, to forgive us the evil we did to you."

Joseph wept when they said these things to him. His brothers fell on their faces before him and said, "Look, we are your servants."

But Joseph said to them, "Don't be afraid. Do I stand in God's place? It is true that you intended evil against me, but God meant it for good to save our people. So don't be afraid; I will take care of you and of your little ones." Thus Joseph comforted them and spoke very fervently to assure them.

Joseph's death (50:22-26):

Joseph continued to live in Egypt, he and his father's family. Joseph lived to be 110 years old, living to see Ephraim's great-grandchildren and Manasseh's grandchildren through Machir. As he was approaching death, Joseph said to his brothers *(family)*, "I am dying, but God will surely come to your rescue, and will bring you up from this land to the land which He swore to give to Abraham, to Isaac, and to Jacob. God will surely take care of you, and you will carry my bones with you when you go up from here." So

Joseph died, and they embalmed him, and he was placed in a coffin *(or sarcophagus)* in Egypt.

Chronology Note

- *According to the reasoning we have done all along about the chronology, Jacob was 91 years older than Joseph.*

- *Since Jacob died at 147, Joseph was 56 years old at the time of Jacob's death.*

- *Joseph lived to be 110. Therefore he lived 54 years after the death of Jacob. It is important to note this length of time.*

Also think about the sequence of events in relation to the famine in Egypt:

- *There were still five years left of the famine when Jacob and his family moved to Egypt (45:11).*

- *Jacob lived a total of seventeen years in Egypt before he died—thus twelve years after the famine ended (47:9,28).*

- *Joseph had been given his high rank in the kingdom in order to accomplish the specific task of saving lives during the famine, so his duties probably ended not long after the famine was over, and the land had returned to prosperity.*

- *He lived 54 years after the death of his father, 66 years after the famine ended.*

- *Obviously he was still counted as an honored man when his father died because the Egyptians showed such concern over his grief for his father.*

- *But due to the time factor alone, it is not surprising that conditions had changed by the time Joseph himself died.*

But note the additional indications that, by the time Joseph died, the political climate of Egypt had changed greatly:

- *He assures his brothers before his death that God would surely visit them, and as it is used here, the word "visit" means to come to their rescue. They were blessed by being given one of* the best parts of the land when they arrived in Egypt, so they did not need "rescuing" at that time.

- There seems to be no thought of carrying Joseph's body back to Canaan at the time of his death—perhaps indicating they would not have been allowed to leave the land for a funeral.

- There is no mention of any mourning on the part of the Egyptians at Joseph's death, even though he had once been a greatly honored man in their midst.

It is as if a curtain closes at the end of the book of Genesis, the scenery changes drastically, and then it opens with the people in slavery by the first verses of Exodus. There is no way to know exactly how much time passes between the end of Genesis and the beginning of Exodus, but remember these indications of a change in the feelings of the Egyptians toward the Israelites that we see here at the end of Genesis.

Selected Bibliography

Church, Alfred J. *Stories of the East from Herodotus.* New York: Dodd, Mead, and Company, n.d. Custance.

Arthur C., *Genesis and Early Man.* Grand Rapids, Michigan: Zondervan Publishing House, 1975.

Davidheiser, Bolton. *Evolution and the Christian Faith.* The Presbyterian Reformed Publishing Company, 1969.

Denton, Michael. *Evolution: Theory in Crisis.* Bethesda, Maryland: Adler & Adler, Publishers, Inc., 1986.

Gish, Duane T. *Challenge of the Fossil Record.* El Cajon, CA: Creation-Life Publishers, 1985.

Keil, Carl, and Delitzsch, Franz. *Biblical Commentary on the Old Testament,* 6 Vols. Keil, "Genesis" (Vol. 1). Reprint. Grand Rapids, MI: Associated Publishers and Authors, Inc., n.d.

Lawrence, T.E. *Seven Pillars of Wisdom.* Atlanta, GA: Communications and Studies, Inc., n.d.

Prichard, James B., (ed.). *The Ancient Near East,* 2 Vols. Princeton, NJ: Princeton University Press, 1975.

Tenny, Merrill C., (ed.). *The Zondervan Pictorial Bible Dictionary.* Grand Rapids, MI: Zondervan Publishing House, 1967.

Waldron, Bob and Sandra. *The History and Geography of the Bible Story.* Fairmont, IN: Guardian of Truth, 1984.

Whitcomb, John C., Jr., and Morris, Henry M. *The Genesis Flood.* Grand Rapids, Michigan: Baker Book House, 1961.

Credits

Graphics credits by page number: **Front Cover**—Earth, moon, and sun: illustration, istockphoto.com; **Page 8**—Cross and clouds: photo, istockphoto.com; **Page 17**—Man studying the Bible: photo, istockphoto.com; **Page 19**—Photos of book covers: photos, designed by Kyle Pope from istockphoto.com images; **Page 21**—Open Bible with "Genesis" blocks: photo, istockphoto.com; **Page 23**—Light shining in the dark: photo, istockphoto.com; **Page 23**—Trees and grasses around a pond: photo, istockphoto.com; **Page 26**—Assorted animals: graphic, istockphoto.com; **Page 28**—Euphrates river from Babylon: photo, istockphoto.com; **Page 30**—Fruit with a bite taken: graphic, istockphoto.com; **Page 32**—Graveyard: photo, istockphoto.com; **Page 37**—Storm clouds over the water: photo, istockphoto.com; **Page 39**—Ark on the water: graphic, public domain; **Page 40**—The mountains of Ararat: photo, istockphoto.com; **Page 42**—Rainbow over mountains and water: photo, istockphoto.com; **Page 45**—The Ancient World: map by Kyle Pope; **Page 47**—The ziggurat of Ur-Nammu: photo, istockphoto.com; **Pages 50-51**—The World of the Patriarchs: map by Kyle Pope; **Page 53**—Modern day Harran: photo, istockphoto.com; **Pages 56-57**—Canaan in the Days of the Patriarchs: map by Kyle Pope; **Page 59**—Modern city of Hebron: photo, istockphoto.com; **Page 63**—Middle-Eastern wild donkey: photo, istockphoto.com; **Page 67**—Barren plain near the Dead Sea: photo, istockphoto.com; **Page 74**—Ruins of ancient Beersheba: photo, Kyle Pope; **Page 76**—"Tomb of the Patriarchs" in Hebron: photo, istockphoto.com; **Page 87**—Possible site of Bethel: photo, public domain; **Page 92**—Mountains of Gilead: photo, Kyle Pope; **Page 97**—Modern city of Nablus: photo, istockphoto.com; **Page 104**—Tel Dothan: photo, Creative Commons, Daniel Ventura; **Page 106**—Camels in front of Giza pyramids: photo, istockphoto.com; **Page 111**—Edfu temple ruins: photo, istockphoto.com; **Page 113**—Tutankhamun statue: photo, istockphoto.com; **Page 116**—Nile Delta: photo, istockphoto.com; **Page 123**—Cave in Hebron: photo, Kyle Pope. **Graphics used throughout the book: Lamp logo:** graphic, unknown public domain; **Compass icon:** graphic, istockphoto.com; **Tree icon:** graphic, istockphoto.com; **Hour glass icon:** graphic, istockphoto.com.